PREACHING

JOB

Preaching Classic Texts

Preaching Apocalyptic Texts
Larry Paul Jones and Jerry L. Sumney

Preaching Job
John C. Holbert

PREACHING

JOB

JOHN C.
HOLBERT

Chalice Press
St. Louis, Missouri

Scripture quotations marked NRSV are from the *New Revised Standard Version Bible*, copyright 1989, Division of Christian Education of the National Council of the Churches of Christ in the USA. Used by permission. All rights reserved. All other scripture translations are author's.

Cover Design: Michael Foley
Cover art: William Blake, "Job Rebuked by his Friends." *Illustrations of the Book of Job*, III, 45, plate 10. The Pierpont Morgan Library/Art Resource, NY.

Art Director: Michael H. Domínguez
Interior design: Wynn Younker

This book is printed on acid-free, recycled paper.

Visit Chalice Press on the World Wide Web at
www.chalicepress.com

10 9 8 7 6 5 4 3 2 1   99 00 01 02 03

Library of Congress Cataloging–in–Publication Data

Holbert, John C.
    Preaching Job / by John C. Holbert.
        p.   cm. -- (Preaching classic texts)
    Includes bibliographical references and index.
    ISBN 0-8272-2959-3
    1. Bible O. T. Job–Commentaries. 2. Bible. O. T. Job–Homiletic use. 3. Bible. O. T. Job–Sermons. 4. Sermons, American. I. Title.   II. Series.
BS14153.3.H65 1999
223'.107–dc21   99-050432
                                                                CIP

CONTENTS

Among the last things that the world appears to need is another commentary on the book of Job. There are so many of them, and so many of those so thorough and valuable, that another one needs to have some sort of uniqueness if it is to justify its existence. I begin with the claim that this one is, in at least certain respects, unique. Its uniqueness arises in four ways.

First, I believe that I have some fresh things to say about the book, both in terms of its content and meaning as well as the ways the author(s) have gone about presenting them.

Second, this book is sent directly to the community of preachers and listeners. These communities include pastors of churches, rabbis of synagogues, and the members of Jewish and Christian congregations who listen to them.

Third, I wish to use the metaphor of drama as a lens through which to witness and to appropriate the book. I do not imply by my use of this metaphor that Job was ever actually performed as a play, although some commentators have suggested that it may have been.[1] But drama has been for me a helpful heuristic device to enable a more lively reading of a story that too often has been seen as an arid philosophical/theological roundtable.

Fourth, because my goal in the book is an eminently practical one, I will include discussion of the several ways that my reading of the book plays itself out in the task of preaching in terms of the content of preaching, the style of preaching, and the rationale for any preaching at all. And I will provide some sermons actually preached, based on the reading. Job, we will find, has a great deal to teach us about preaching.

In these four ways, then, I think this commentary to be unique. In such a brief book, full attention to the astonishingly complex linguistic dilemmas thrown up by the Hebrew text of Job can, of course, not be addressed in any sort of detail. Only the most important linguistic dilemmas, those that significantly affect the understanding of a given passage, will be addressed. Unless otherwise marked, the translations of the book of Job are my own.

This book has been long in coming. I wanted to do it right after the completion of my dissertation of 1975. But what a mistake that would have been! In the intervening years I have: been a pastor of a fast-growing church, been and still am a longtime husband, become a father of two now-grown children, been the interim pastor of a huge church riven with crisis, an interim pastor of another large one, and taught at two institutions of higher learning, the last of which I am still part. These summary experiences of my adult life do not, of course, reveal those uncountable events and people that have made me the person I now am. I can readily say I am not now what I once was.

And through these many life experiences Job has both whispered and shouted to me like the ghost of Hamlet's father, "Remember me!" And I have. Old Job has never been very far from my mind during the experiences recounted above. But, it must be said, it has seldom been the same Job whom I have conjured up or who, on occasion, has arisen on his own. I first had to reckon with Job the revolutionary satirist, the strident mocker of the God who seemed to be mismanaging the universe. Then Job the agonized sufferer floated into my head, bringing his pathetic demands for truth to his wretched friends and his apparently angry, and finally uncaring, God. And there was always the pious Job of pulpit and pew, who ultimately saw his God and converted in a blaze of religious fervor. As little as I could see such a Job as that latter one during any of my readings, he certainly had a firm grip on the hearts of many in the communities of faith to whom I spoke. And now there is my Job of today, who may partake of a little of each of these former manifestations. But that Job needs to arise from the reading found in these pages, and, I will suggest, it is that Job who needs to be preached and taught and prayed with in the community as we enter a new millennium.

An author has more debts than can ever be repaid by some dry list of names. But here goes. Foremost is my mentor, now colleague, Professor W. J. A. Power, whose early obsession with Job he kindly infected me with; because of him, I remain diseased (in the most literal sense). It was in a year-long seminar on the book in 1970–71 that Bill first infected me. I should then thank Norman Habel, whose wonderful 1985 commentary perhaps reinfected me, not least by having close acquaintance with and some appreciation for my unpublished and obscure dissertation, a heady and astonishing fact. And there is my wife of thirty years, Reverend Diana B. Holbert, who put up with that dissertation so long ago and now, with her own wonderful ministry and an empty nest at home, finds herself still sharing her husband with the old loudmouth from Uz. She, unlike Job's so-called friends, knows well that "to withhold kindness from a friend is to forsake the fear of Shaddai." For her long friendship and her sustaining love, I thank her and dedicate this little book to her. Here it is at last, my love. You, more than anyone else, have given me the right ears with which to hear what I think Job is trying to say. Thanks.

CHAPTER 1

The Prologue (Job 1—2)

Before any serious use of the book of Job can be made in the community of faith, it is essential that the *whole* book be read. Please note that I said the whole book. I am fully aware of the enormous literature that surrounds the apparently complex compilation of the forty-two chapters of our canonical Job, but I have no intention of repeating, evaluating, or summarizing that work. (Interested readers may consult any of the standard commentaries for learned speculation about the origin and structure of the book we have before us.) I plan to read Job 1–42 here. We have no early witnesses to any other Job than the forty-two-chapter one we see in our modern translations. It is true that the Septuagint, the fourth-to-third-century C.E. Greek translation of the Hebrew text, is substantially shorter as a whole, while occasionally longer in some parts, than the Hebrew text we know, but it too has exactly forty-two chapters. My commentary will read those chapters, and the reader may follow the commentary with any modern translation. In fact, I recommend that the reader have a translation in hand, because I do not propose, for reasons of space, to reproduce much of the text. I will, however, comment extensively on certain verses while saying little or nothing about others. All translations in the book are my own. My goal in the commentary is to read Job in such a way as to provide the reader a clear sense of the whole in order that the meanings of the whole may be illustrated and illuminated.

Job 1:1–5

The story begins with a heavily stylized folktale. The opening verse gives the reader several bits of extremely important information, all of which will play significant roles in the unfolding drama. First, four adjectival phrases delineate the character of the hero. He is *tam*, a word whose semantic range includes completeness, innocence, wholeness, that which is in accordance with the truth (cf. Am. 5:10; Judg. 9:16, 19; Josh. 24:14; 2 Sam. 15:11). And he is *yashar*, the physical meaning of which is level or straight, with the extended meaning of straightforward, just, and upright. This latter word is regularly found in materials influenced by the Deuteronomic writers to describe those persons and things that are thought to be right or pleasing in the eyes of God (cf. Ex. 15:26; 1 Kings 11:33, 38; 2 Kings 10:30; Jer. 34:15). Both of these adjectives are heavily loaded; any person so described could be nothing less than a model of religious and ethical virtue. And if the two words are translated together as an example of hendiadys, a single concept expressed by two linked words, we might read "perfectly upright" or "absolutely blameless." It will be well for the reader to remember these two words; they will appear several more times in the tale with some surprising and telling implications. In sum, the very first thing we are told about Job is that he is a supremely religious and virtuous man, a pious paragon of mythical proportion.

And two more descriptions enhance the portrait. Job "fears God" and "shuns evil." The former phrase is ubiquitous in the Hebrew Bible (cf. among many others Neh. 5:9, 15; Gen. 42:18; Ex. 1:17, 21; Deut. 25:18; Ps. 55:19). Most especially in the wisdom traditions, the "fear of God" stands as the "beginning of wisdom" (Ps. 111:10; Prov. 9:10, though the actual phrase in those passages is "fear of YHWH"). To fear God in the Bible is to act in such a way as to be wise, to place oneself among those who, like trees, are planted near streams of water (Ps. 1), who are blessed and loved by God. The last phrase, "shuns evil," repeats a thought found often in wisdom texts (cf. Prov. 3:7; 13:19; 16:6, 17; Ps. 34:14; 37:27). In the latter two passages, the psalmists urge their hearers to "shun evil and do good." Clearly,

Job has spent a lifetime doing precisely that. Job 28:28 will claim that "the fear of the Lord is wisdom and the shunning of evil is understanding." The story's narrator has begun with a description of a hero who has precisely and completely fulfilled the requirements of correct behavior in order to gain wisdom and understanding. At least some tradition in Israel has claimed this fact to be true. Perhaps one of the story's concerns will be to determine in what ways Job has gained wisdom and understanding and if such wisdom and understanding do, in fact, follow from such right behaviors.

This Job is certainly fantastically pious and also fantastically rich, truly larger than life, a man worthy of the accolade "greatest." But what of the character of the man, his behavior toward his children? The next three verses describe again an exemplary series of actions.

His wonderful children are fond of parties and would never think of excluding any of their siblings, not even the girls, from the festivities. But after every one of these feasts, without fail, Job was the first one at the door of the church the next morning, ready to offer ten whole burnt offerings, one for each of the children, because Job was afraid that "perhaps my children sinned and cursed[1] God in their hearts [i.e., silently or secretly]." Job did this always. This quite remarkable behavior on Job's part in verse 5 is worthy of a closer look.

It is, on the surface, extraordinarily religious. After every feast, attended by all ten of his children, Job heads for the place of sacrifice to offer up holocausts for each one of them. This is not only quite expensive, the behavior of a very wealthy man, but it is also inordinately time-consuming: ten burnt offerings at least ten times a year. And why? Job fears that one of his children just might have cursed God privately, might have thought an untoward thought, might have had an unvoiced negative idea about something God would find sinful. Hence the costly rivers of blood and the smoking meat. What sort of man is it who acts in such a way? Is it a man content with his life and his relationship with his God? Or is it a man who is consumed with the possibilities of what might go wrong, what could go wrong, what in the course of time usually does go wrong? What sort of God is it who needs such lavish propitiation to hold off the ever-ready divine rebuke? In what way more exactly does Job "fear God"? However one answers these questions at this early place in the story, the relationship between Job and his God comes to the fore here and will be one of the major issues of the tale. We will have occasion to return to that relationship again and again.

Job 1:6–12

The scene shifts to the divine world, and two divine beings are introduced. As the council of the gods gathers, the Satan appears. It is important for a reader of this story to note that this figure is *the* Satan; Satan is not his name but his title. He is "the adversary" or "the accuser." In modern parlance, he might be a prosecuting attorney, charged with the responsibility of careful observation of human behavior and its evaluation before the court. This role is derived from the various places the noun occurs in the Hebrew Bible (cf. Num. 22:22, 32; 1 Sam. 29:4; 2 Sam. 19:22; 1 Kings 11:14, 23, 25). Only in Job, Zechariah, and 1 Chronicles is the Satan thought of as superhuman, although the angel who confronts Balaam and his donkey in Numbers is himself called an adversary; but there he is sent expressly by God to waylay the prophet who is about to curse Israel.

The council assembles, and YHWH, who is clearly the leader of the council, addresses the Satan in what sounds like stylized language. "Where have you come from?" The Satan responds, "From roaming the earth, walking around on it." The Satan's answer suggests his role in the council; he observes the affairs of human beings and reports back at the instigation of YHWH and the council. "Have you set your heart on Job?" asks YHWH. "There is no one like him on earth! He is a man *tam* and *yashar*, who fears God and shuns evil." YHWH quotes the narrator of verse 1 exactly, reinforcing the apparent fabulous piety of Job.

The Satan is less than impressed. "For no reason does Job fear God?" In other words, asks the Satan, is not Job pious for some reason or other? Do you really think that Job would act as he does with no expectation of reward or payment of some kind? The word "nothing" can mean either literally no "thing," no tangible gift (so Gen. 29:15), or "for no reason or purpose" (so Mal. 1:10). The Satan apparently emphasizes the former meaning, because he goes on to accuse YHWH of protecting Job's person, his house, and all that he has; his works are blessed, his possessions enormous. However, the other possible meaning of the word will also be important to the prologue. The Satan challenges YHWH to stretch out the divine hand and "touch all that he has." The result, says the Satan, will be a loud and angry curse.

The Satan has put his adverserial hand on a very important question: Is there such a thing as disinterested piety? Do I not worship God for some particular reward, whether it be material (a BMW at the crassest level), personal (I feel so much better when I go to church–hardly less crass), or spiritual (I hope to win heaven thereby–any less crass?). Is it genuinely possible for anyone to fear God for nothing save pure love of God? Might this be another important theme for our story?

Job has in fact been very interested in certain of his possessions, particularly his children and their possible secret sins. The Satan has raised the question that arose for us when we read verse 5; perhaps Job doth protest too much with his extraordinary sacrificial behavior? Is he too attached to his things? Is he so untrusting of his God as to spend the bulk of his time burning gifts to that God so as to keep God at bay, away from his possessions? The Satan and we and now YHWH would like to know. "All right! Everything that he has is in your power; only do not stretch out your hand to him." The Satan has asked for God's hand to be "stretched out" against Job, but in response God has demanded that the Satan not "stretch out" his hand against him.

What are we to make of God's behavior here? Commentators have long spoken of a wager, a kind of bet between God and the Satan. That is not quite accurate. There is no bet here. If it were, there would be a specified reward; someone would win a pot with something specific in it. This is not a bet, but it is a test. YHWH has held Job up as the very model of a divine servant, boasting to the Satan, in effect, that if there were more like him, the Satan might be out of work. But the Satan retorts that God has not looked closely enough at this so-called paragon of piety. He acts well and righteously precisely because he is rich and comfortable. Change that fact, and you will see Job's true colors. And God is plainly interested in such a test, and who better to try it on than the wonderful Job?

But back to the question: What are we to make of God? Some have spoken of God's cruelty, manipulating the life of the world's most faithful servant, pulling the strings of a soon-to-be battered puppet, all to discover whether God is really loved and worshiped only for God's own self. Archibald MacLeish certainly heard it like that in his Pulitzer Prize–winning play, *JB*.[2] In scene two, Mr. Zuss (*aka* God) and Nickles (*aka* the Satan) are engaged in a heated debate about the meaning of JB's suffering. Zuss says:

> Isn't there anything you understand?
> It's from the ash heap God is seen
> Always! Always from the ashes.
> Every saint and martyr knew that.

Nickles sneers his response:

> And so he suffers to see God:
> Sees God because he suffers. Beautiful!

Zuss demands that Nickles cover his face with the masks they both carry, and Nickles says:

> …a human
> Face would shame the mouth that said that!

For Nickles, any claim that suffering is the way to see God best is monstrous and callous. Thus, MacLeish's character finds God cruel.

But that is not the only way to evaluate the test. If we rule out of the story the presupposition that God is omniscient—there is no claim to that belief—then the test is a real one, not a cruel game. God wants to know whether or not God's human creation worships for reward alone. Perhaps a helpful analogy may be found in the harrowing story of Genesis 22 and the near-sacrifice of Isaac, the child of the promise. It is apparently crucial to that story that God know whether Abraham trusts the God of the promise or the physical manifestation of the promise, his son, Isaac.[3] The test is real; God does not know the outcome, as the details of the story make clear. By hearing the story in this way, I do not wish to lessen the very real pain that each of these stories brings. Neither Abraham's test nor Job's test is a source of great comfort to me, but I think it goes too far to accuse God of simple cruelty or sadism by pursuing the tests.

What the reader is introduced to, then, is the question of the nature of God. This, I think, is the primary question of the book of Job, namely, who is God? And the book's possible answer(s) to that question may itself cast doubt on other answers given to the question in Israelite tradition.

Job 1:13–22

The Satan leaves the council chamber and heads toward Job's huge estate. In four hammer-blows of increasing disaster Job is told by four successive survivors that his oxen, donkeys and servants, his sheep and more servants, his camels and the remainder of his servants, and all ten of his sons and daughters have been stolen or exterminated. The means of these multiple slaughters are worthy of note. The oxen and donkeys are taken and the servants killed by marauding Sabeans. This act of human theft and murder is followed by "a fire of God" falling from the sky, consuming both sheep and servants. The third disaster is again a human one. The perpetrators this time are the Chaldeans, who, like the Sabeans, steal the livestock and murder the servants. The fourth, and greatest, tragedy is the death of all ten of Job's children as the result of a "great wind" that strikes "the four corners of the house" where Job's children are celebrating one of their regular feasts.

The alternating of human and natural/supernatural devices suggests that the Satan has at his disposal the whole arsenal of God with which to conduct the test. The reader waits anxiously for Job's reactions to these horrific events. Those who witnessed the extraordinary description of a pious Job at the beginning of the tale are far from disappointed. In classic actions of Middle

Eastern mourning, Job arises, ritually tears his outer robe, shaves his head, and falls on the ground in the proper posture of worship. He then recites words clearly well known to him and to any who know the traditions of the faith of Israel (1:21). And the narrator concludes this remarkable confession with the comment, "In all this Job did not sin nor did he ascribe any worthless thing to God." Two parts of this sentence are worthy of comment.

The "all this" apparently includes the four disasters and Job's reaction to them. No one, the narrator announces, could possibly accuse Job of reacting to the hand he had been dealt in any but the most pious and laudatory ways. That is what the narrator means, we can suppose, when he claims that Job "did not sin" in any way by his response. The most basic meaning of this word for "sin" is "to miss the target." Job has definitely scored a bull's-eye with his pious poem, according to our storyteller.

The second part of the sentence is more difficult. The problem is the meaning of the word I have translated "a worthless thing." This word occurs only three times in the entire Hebrew Bible, only one of those outside of Job (see Jer. 23:13). A related noun (see Job 6:7 and Lam. 2:14) describes things that are insipid or tasteless, the Job passage referring to food and the Lamentations passage referring to visions of false prophets.

This brief review of the meager evidence for the meaning of this word can at least lead us to reject the NRSV's translation, "wrong-doing." The *result* of something that is "worthless" may be wrong, but it is the act itself that is empty or worthless. Hence, the narrator tells us that by speaking as Job has in response to the four extraordinary disasters that have happened to him, he has never charged that God has done anything that could be labeled worthless or empty. Why has the narrator planted such a notion in our minds? How could Job's apparently pious poem suggest to us that God might have acted in an empty or worthless way?

Is it possible that God's test of Job is in fact somehow empty and worthless? Is the poem anything more than a piece of religious doggerel, trotted out on those occasions when inexplicable and unspeakable things happen to perfectly wonderful people, nice phrases uttered to provide some semblance of rationality in the face of the irrational? We all know these sorts of phrases: "Time heals all wounds" or "God wanted her more than you did." One possible reason that the narrator has claimed that Job did not charge God with empty and worthless actions is that we, the readers, are in fact quite ready to believe that that is precisely what God in fact *has* done. The terrible test of Job, on the face of it, appears to be quite worthless, and the fact that Job does not call it so merely serves to emphasize its worthlessness.

So, where are we at the end of the first chapter? Job is bereft of nearly all of the outer manifestations of his former glory. His livestock are stolen, his servants and children all dead. He has reacted with overt religiosity, something we might expect from a man who has spent an inordinate amount of his life sacrificing rich offerings just in case his wonderful children might silently have cursed God. And the rewards of such exemplary activity? Silent fields, the only sound that of familiar words spoken into a blasted landscape of destruction and death. Are we to see this man as exemplary? Or do we long for him to forgo his platitudes and fill the air with painful truth, perhaps the truth that the God he has spent so long propitiating and serving has inexplicably turned against him, as far as he can see? Of course, we have a different perspective. We know that it is the test that has cost Job his familiar life, not the unexplainable anger or rage of God. We need to watch Job closely now, but, also, we need to watch God. Both characters present complex portraits that demand careful attention.

Job 2:1–8

The scene returns to the heavenly court. The opening verse is nearly identical to its counterpart (1:6) in the first heavenly council, but there is one addition. The Satan, in the first encounter, is described as being merely "among" his fellow divine beings. Now he explicitly comes among them "to present himself before YHWH." He has done his work with Job in fulfillment of the terms of the test, and he appears to be anxious to discuss the results. After an exact repetition of the initial exchange of 1:8 in 2:3, YHWH again draws the Satan's attention to the remarkable servant, Job, and adds to the phrase what amounts to a claim of victory in the test. "He still holds fast his integrity, though you incited me against him to swallow him for no reason" (2:3). This divine statement is worthy of some comment.

The Satan has said that if Job were to lose all of his material wealth, he would curse YHWH in the face. Job was described both by the narrator and by YHWH as a man *tam* and *yashar* (1:1, 8; 2:3). The adjective *tam* is from the same verbal root as the word in 2:3 translated "integrity." The Satan claims that Job's integrity is the direct result of his wealth and ease. YHWH triumphantly announces that the test has proven the Satan wrong. Job's integrity remains intact; he has in fact not cursed YHWH. However, the final word of YHWH's triumphant cry is disturbing. At 1:9, the Satan had founded his call for the test of Job on the belief that Job was not a man of piety "for no reason." On the contrary, he was rich; that is why he was seemingly pious and God-fearing. Now YHWH borrows the Satan's word of challenge and uses it to accuse the Satan of having incited YHWH to swallow Job "for no reason." What can YHWH mean by saying that? Is the test finally meaningless to YHWH? YHWH seemed vitally interested in discovering whether or not Job was a genuinely faithful servant. YHWH's use of the word "for no reason" seems incongruous in the light of that apparent interest.

The narrator's odd statement at the end of chapter 1 that Job did not charge God with any worthless act throws a possibly interesting light on YHWH's use of the Satan's word. If we, the readers, are perhaps ready to call this entire test a worthless act, could we not hear YHWH's statement as some kind of admission that the test was indeed worthless, performed for no defensible reason? Might not, then, the whole dialogue between YHWH and the Satan be, in the last analysis, for no reason, worthless? If so, the question of the nature of God and God's ways in the world is a very live one at this point in the drama.

Or is there still another possible way to read the phrase? Is YHWH tweaking the Satan by using his own word? The Satan's claim that Job's piety was quite false, based only on wealth, has apparently been proven wrong, and YHWH's use of the word is part of the gloating of the victor. In paraphrase, it might be: "So, you said there was no reason for Job's piety, huh? Well, what really has no reason, no genuine purpose, is your attempt to incite me to destroy him. I have won, and that is what finally counts! The test is over!" But, as far as the Satan is concerned, the test is not yet complete.

To YHWH's shout of victory, the Satan responds with what appears to be a further test. "Skin for skin! Everything that a man has he will give for his life!" This proverbial phrase has engendered enormous comment, but David Clines has offered a neat solution to the difficulty of understanding.[4] "Skin for skin" refers to a bartering situation wherein something is given in exchange for something of similar value. The Satan is referring to a possible future exchange between Job and YHWH. If YHWH attacks Job's very life, the Satan predicts that Job will, in return, attack the very life of God in the only way a human can attack the deity–by cursing. In other words, the "skin" of God's attack on Job's life will be answered by the "skin" of Job's curse. This is so, the Satan insists, because "everything a man possesses he will give for his life." The test has not gone far enough. "Touch his bone and his flesh; he will curse your face!" And YHWH agrees. But if the test is to have any real meaning, Job cannot die. He must suffer, but he must not die. "Guard his life," YHWH warns the Satan.

So, the Satan strikes Job with the disease of the sixth plague of Egypt (Ex. 9:9–11), foul boils that cloak his entire body. Job grabs a broken piece of pottery with which to scrape his putrid ulcers, and he sits down on a heap of ashes. Those with repulsive skin diseases were separated from the community and often found themselves living among the garbage. Job's famous ash heap may be the ancient equivalent of a modern landfill, with its ripe smells and continuous burning.

Job 2:9–13

Into this blasted scene steps Job's wife. What she says to her husband has been the subject of much debate. "Are you still holding on to your integrity? Curse God, and die." In her first sentence she precisely echoes YHWH's retort to the Satan at 2:3. By using the same expression, the reader may assume that she has the same understanding of the key word *integrity* that YHWH has. *Integrity* here appears to mean a refusal to allow any calamity, no matter how appalling, to bring one to curse God. Both for YHWH and Job's wife, the claim that Job is *tam* means that he is a man who would never curse God, no matter what. Observing her husband in agony, bereft of all material benefits, reduced to a so-called life on a fetid refuse heap, she urges him to reject that integrity by cursing God in order that he might die. She has been accused of shrewish behavior here, or even of being the tool of the Satan, but her motivation for speaking as she does may be compassion for her suffering spouse. Whatever that motivation may be, the important point is that the direct connection between cursing God and dying is made. Indeed, both the Satan and Job's wife assume a certain relationship between the action of God-cursing and dying. It will prove to be significant to the story to understand what it might mean to curse God, so we will need to return to the issue again.

At last, three friends of Job, after hearing of "all this evil that had come upon him," arrange to meet and travel together to him with the express purpose of "showing sympathy for him" and "comforting him." But when they arrive in the vicinity of the sufferer, seeing him from a considerable distance, they immediately begin the rites of deepest mourning. They do not even recognize their friend, so marred is his appearance. They lift their voices in a great weeping and tear their outer garments. Commonly in the Hebrew Bible, at this point in the mourning ritual, the mourner would now sit in ashes. We could imagine that Job's friends would join him on his own heap. Instead, they do something not easy to understand. "They scattered dust upon their heads heavenward."

Once again, one is reminded of the sixth plague of Egypt (Ex. 9:8–10). Job's disease is the boils of that plague, but the way the boils were created was the act of Moses "scattering dust heavenward." As the dust settled on humans and animals, the boils were created. Are the friends using a kind of sympathetic magic to identify fully with the pain and suffering of their friend? In other words, if he has the boils, we may at least metaphorically get them too. Or is their act, on the contrary, a way to ward off the evil that has befallen him? Are they rather separating themselves from him, not wishing to be contaminated by the obvious evil that has appeared? Their act of throwing dust into the air would then be a way of avoiding the evil of the boils.

Their final act in the prologue could be a clue to the meaning of the dust throwing. They sit in absolute silence with him on the ground. This silence, we are told, is the result of their seeing "that his pain was very great." This silence has often been seen as a great act of compassion, dear friends sitting around the bed of affliction, waiting patiently to see if they can be of any help. That is, however, not the only way to understand the silence. The actions of the friends, including their extraordinarily long silence, are all typical actions of those mourning for the dead. Could it be that Job's three friends lament the virtual death of Job, having decided on seeing him that he is well beyond any hope of life? Their silence is not then purely sympathetic, but is a silence engendered by the presence of a dead man.

Job's three friends, who embarked on a mission of sympathy and comfort, have, in the presence of the once-mighty Job, begun the rites of mourning—expansive weeping, the tearing of their expensive outer garments, the grandiose scattering of dust on their heads, all followed by a superhuman seven-day-and-seven-night silence. As far as they are concerned, their friend is dead, and, as they will soon say over and over, deservedly so. But, to their horror, they will find that Job is far from dead, although at the beginning of the long discussion he wishes he were. It is, however, not his only wish as he shatters the extraordinary silence with equally extraordinary words.

Comment

There are at least three purposes for the prologue.

(1) *A literary purpose.* Without the prologue the ensuing plot is very different indeed. Without it, when the friends and Job square off about the origin and meaning of Job's disasters, the reader has no way to adjudicate the debate. It would merely

be Job's word against theirs. But after reading the prologue, I am clearly cognizant of one important fact: Job is not a sinner. Quite the opposite appears to be true. Job, by the narrator's lights and by YHWH's own claims, is the earth's most religious creature, and because of that fact he is chosen for the test. The prologue becomes a classic example of dramatic irony: The reader is allowed to see certain events and overhear certain conversations to which some of the characters of the story are not privy. This literary device, among other things, affords great pleasure to the reader who may ride above the fray of the debate, possessed of inside knowledge that allows privileged evaluation to occur. As we witness the debate, the words and events of the prologue forever color our measure of the struggle.

(2) *A theological purpose.* The question of the nature and purpose of God is very much alive as we conclude the prologue. Just what sort of God is this who enters into the test of this God's most faithful servant? Just why is this God so interested in discovering whether the faithful servant worships God for no other purpose than that God is worthy of such worship? Clearly, this God is not the God of classical theology, not omniscient, not impassable, not omnicompetent. This God wants to know some things that are apparently not currently known. Because this God falls silent for the next thirty-six chapters, the reader will have to wait a very long time to address these questions again.

(3) *An anthropological purpose.* Job and his friends are introduced to us in the prologue, but their introduction is more than a literary device, although it obviously is that too. At the end of the prologue, I am uncertain about the words and actions of every one of these four characters. Job's piety, loudly trumpeted by God and the narrator, seems absurdly excessive, as he spends his days at the altar, propitiating his God for the possible and secret sins of his ten children who by any standard appear exemplary in the story. Is Job a man of great piety or a man of great fear, wondering if the God who has gifted him is ever anxious to take it all away for the smallest of reasons—or perhaps for no reason at all? And the friends. Are their actions in the presence of the sufferer done to console and comfort, as the narrator tells us was the purpose of their journey to

Job's estate, or are they so repulsed and terrified when they actually see him that they begin the mourning rites for the dead, treating him as one already and rightfully deceased? These are literary questions of character, but they lead to broader anthropological questions.

What is the proper way in which a human being should be related to God? That is, how should we act in the face of God; what does God actually require of us? And a related question is: How should we act in relation to one another, especially in the face of enormous and inexplicable suffering? And how should the sufferer act when confronted by such suffering? What is the proper human stance in suffering?

All of these questions are raised in the prologue of Job. Perhaps the simplest evaluation of the prologue is that it whets our appetites for whatever discussion is to follow.

CHAPTER 2

Job 3

It has quite regularly been said that chapters 1–2 and chapter 3ff. must be the work of two different authors.[1] The reasoning goes: The pious Job of the prologue can hardly be this angry, blasphemous, vituperative orator who appears to shatter the silence at the end of chapter 2. Of course, such an argument only holds if the assumption of Job's unshakable piety is accepted. But if the portrayal is more multivalent, as I have suggested, then the angry Job is not unlikely at all. The key connecting verse is 3:25. "No doubt, the great fear I greatly feared has come upon me; that which I dreaded has happened to me." I have translated the first part of the sentence awkwardly to capture the literal sense. The fact that Job's worst fears have been all too terribly realized in his life is nothing else than the manifestation of those fears that led him to the endless round of sacrifices in the prologue. He begins his powerful and lengthy lament with the apparent conviction that someone has done something terrible, so terrible that all of his sacrifices have not sufficed to stave off the disaster. What he feared, namely, the swift and inexorable assault of the deity in response to some human wickedness, has happened. In the face of the horror Job is lamenter, complainer, and questioner all at the same time.

The speech of chapter 3 is nothing else than a creation in reverse. "May the day in which I was born die, along with the night that said, 'A male child is conceived!'" Job quickly establishes the tone of his opening outburst of the dialogue. It is no simple cry for death, no "I wish I'd never been born." What Job demands is the disappearance of his birthday along with the night when he was conceived by his parents; what he requests is that the day and night that saw his joyous birth and his rapturous conception drop out of the pages of history, slip from the calendar of the years. The inspiration of this astonishing plea is clearly Genesis 1.[2]

In verses 4–5 Job commands that the day become night, in effect turning God's creative work around. In fact, verse 4 literally repeats and reverses God's creative act as Job says, "That day! Let there be darkness!" Job thus usurps the power of God, borrowing God's words and grammar in a kind of perverse act of de-creation. Verses 6–8 continue the destructive commands, as Job shouts for the night to be seized by the thickest darkness, then returns to the command form of God's creation, saying "Look at that night! Let there be barrenness!" In verse 8 Job calls on certain magicians, "day-cursers" he names them, to curse the night. These magicians will have to be very powerful to bring an end to a day and a night that have already been, so Job insists that his magicians will be able to "stir up Leviathan." This is not the last time in the book of Job that someone will be challenged to "stir up Leviathan" (41:10).[3]

In verses 11ff. Job shifts his demands. If he had to be born at all, why did he not die at birth, be stillborn? If so, he would now find himself in Sheol, that shadowy place in Hebrew thinking that finally claimed all persons, whether they be good, bad, short, tall, fat, thin. All went to Sheol, a place to be avoided as long as possible. But the wretched Job sees Sheol as a place of "quiet," where "the wicked cease their troubling and the weary rest" (v. 17). But the quiet and rest of Sheol, filled as it is with kings and paupers and everyone in between, are denied to the blasted Job, who at the end of his outcry turns noticeably philosophical.

Job asks the "why" question, beginning at verse 20. "Why is light given to one in misery, or life to a bitter one?" Job's life is so appalling, so empty, so hopeless, that he can see no reason why God would give him the light of life when death and nonexistence would be so much sweeter. He extends his question at verse 23. "Why light for one whose path is hidden, one whom God has hedged round?" The word *hedged* calls to mind the prologue where the Satan employed the same word (spelled slightly differently–1:10) to accuse God of protecting Job so well that of course Job would sing God's praises. Taking the hedge away precipitates the test. Job now cries that the hedge of God is not a protective one but a restrictive one, binding him in ignorance of the true meaning and purpose of a life that by all appearances has neither purpose nor meaning.

The last verse of the monologue hilariously sets up the spoken entrance of Job's long-silent friends. "I am not at ease, not quiet; I have no rest. Trouble comes" (3:26). Job's use of "trouble" reminds the reader of Job's desire to be in Sheol where the "wicked cease troubling" (3:17). The surest sign that Job is not in Sheol is the grand entrance of Eliphaz. The wicked may not trouble in Sheol, but we are still very much on Earth, in a pile of ashes to be exact, and for Job, Eliphaz will prove to be nothing but trouble.

Comment

The proverbial patience of Job has lasted, at best, for two chapters. His outburst of rage, confusion, and furious demands has brought to light the fears that his outwardly comfortable circumstances in the prologue served to mask. The "fear he feared" and the thing "he dreaded" have happened in spades. His life has been reduced to ashes and shards, the residue of a fiery cataclysm. Job has decided not to take his tragedy lying down, but chooses to shout his protests loudly and clearly to anyone who will hear. Though the basic desire Job expresses in this speech is for death, there is more than that which motivates him. Though his life of exemplary piety ought to have led him to ease and comfort, satisfaction and rest, he instead is beset by "trouble." In response, he first asks that the day of his birth and the night of his conception both be cursed in order that they might disappear forever, never to have been at all (3:3–10). But, since he has unfortunately been born, he then wishes that he had died at birth (3:11–12, 16), with the pleasant result that he would even now be in Sheol, a place of peace and tranquility where all find ultimate rest and freedom from trouble, turmoil, and confusion (3:13–15, 17–19).

At the end of the speech, Job turns to that confusion. He is experiencing the most painful of cognitive dissonances, where long-held expectations are not being fulfilled while unexpected and unexplained horrors have taken control. This dissonance leads to the anguished question, "Why?" Job's "why" takes a twofold form. The broader question is the first one. "Why am I, so miserable and so bitter, alive at all? What possible purpose could a life like this one have?" The second part of the "why" is: "Why am I, who cannot understand, or, better, who is prevented from understanding by God, alive at all?" The first question is filled with pure anguish, while the second is urged by the deep curiosity so endemic to the human spirit. In the long dialogue about to begin, the spirit of the latter question will eventually triumph over the despair of the former.

Chapter 3 starts the dialogue with a cry of pain coupled with a demand for some answers, both hurled into a universe seemingly gone mad. Job's friends, deeply affected by Job's scathing words, now reveal their own theological concerns as they begin their lengthy attempts both to convict the sinner and to turn him back to the right path, the path from whence he has so obviously strayed.[4]

A few comments before we start the dialogue. As we listen to the four friends of Job, I will ask three questions of them in the attempt to discern their similarities to and differences from one another in their approaches to Job, as well as to surmise how that discernment leads to a careful determination of the look of each one. I mean "look" both in a metaphorical and a physical sense. Though the poem of Job has often been described as an intellectual duel or a theological debate, I believe that the poet has given the reader many clues whereby the characters take on quite discernable and describable personas. And unless the reader can actually "see" each one as the dialogue is read, the result will be a disengagement from the very real human level of the discussion. These are *people* who are talking, and they need to be seen as such.

The three questions are:

1. What exactly is the basic thrust of the argument of each speech? Where is the central verse, or verses, that best characterize that thrust?
2. What are the key examples of the dialogue technique described in note 4? How do those examples illustrate the basic thrust of question 1?
3. If I were costuming each speaker for a dramatic presentation of the dialogue, what would each speaker wear and why? How might the costume add to the force and intent of the dialogue?

The answers to these questions should help us both discern the ideas of the debate and delineate and personify the debaters, adding a level of human reality to the engagement.

The First Cycle (Job 4—14)

Eliphaz is the first to respond to the Joban outburst of chapter 3. The reader has certain expectations of Eliphaz, since he has been called a "friend" of the sufferer. We are anxious to hear what the friend Eliphaz will say, he who has journeyed so far to see his friend and who has sat silently for seven days and nights near the ash heap.

The opening line is important to catch the tone of Eliphaz' response (v. 2).

The first verb out of Eliphaz' mouth speaks of a test. This verb is used in some very significant places in the Hebrew Bible. God tests Abraham with the demand to kill his son on Mount Moriah (Gen. 22:1), and God puts the people of Israel to the test in the wilderness by demanding that they heed the divine voice and faithfully follow the statutes and ordinances of God, thereby avoiding the diseases that fell upon the Egyptians (Ex. 15:25). In the same way that God tested God's servants and some of those servants tested God, so now Eliphaz proposes to test Job with a word.

Is it not ironic that Eliphaz announces his test by asking whether or not Job will be "impatient" as a result? The word he uses can also mean "weary," and the effect of Eliphaz' words will create both impatience and weariness in Job. The irony also arises when we remember the proverbial "patience of Job." Surely chapter 3's deeply felt cries have ended whatever patience Job may have had. Yet Job's first friend is, he says, unable to restrain his words. This, as we shall see, is a gross understatement. Eliphaz' words come in a torrent; restraint is not a trait that can be ascribed to Eliphaz. But at the outset, he urges Job not to be impatient.

The test of Eliphaz' word then begins (vv. 3–5). He reminds Job of his past good works, where he has disciplined, strengthened, and supported those around him who were especially in need of such ministrations. Now Job is the one in need of firming up, and instead of heeding his own good advice so readily dished up by the comfortable Job, the now-fallen Job is instead "impatient" and "disturbed." It is clear from Eliphaz' use of those two adjectives what he thinks of the Joban monologue of chapter 3; Job has obviously failed the test of the disasters that have come his way, precisely because he has become impatient and disturbed, Eliphaz' summary words for Job's first speech. But Job's initial failure can still be corrected if he passes the test that Eliphaz is about to administer (vv. 6–7).

These verses are the heart of Eliphaz' opening speech, and the nouns he chooses are each crucial for his meaning. The word *fear* is often rendered "awe" and on occasion "worship." The reader will remember that Job has three times in the prologue (1:1, 8; 2:3) been called one who "fears YHWH." And the two nouns translated "integrity" in verse 6 and "upright" in verse 7 are two other descriptions of Job given thrice in the same verses of the prologue. By choosing just these three nouns Eliphaz makes the following claim: A true believer can rely completely on "fear, integrity, and uprightness" to avoid destruction and to live in hope.

Immediately, the reader senses a serious problem with Eliphaz' claim. He has upbraided Job for giving in to impatience and disturbance in response to the cruel events of his life. The implication is that no person who possesses genuine fear, integrity, and uprightness need ever fear destruction or the loss of hope. But Job has indeed shown evidence of loss of hope and deep disturbance as a result of near complete destruction of the life he has known. One could well summarize the content of his opening speech as a loss of hope and a deep disturbance. Hence, for Eliphaz, Job can have no genuine fear, integrity, or uprightness. But, unbeknownst to Eliphaz, those three words are precisely the ones used to characterize Job in the prologue; both the narrator and YHWH (twice) say so.

What then is the reader to conclude? Either the narrator of the prologue and YHWH are not to be trusted, or Eliphaz is seriously in error concerning his conclusions about his friend. Eliphaz' error becomes clear very quickly. He may think he is offering Job some sage advice, gleaned, as we shall soon see, from a high and holy place, but in fact he is blithering on in the face of facts he knows nothing of. His advice is in effect a cruel assault on his suffering friend, who *is* a person characterized by "fear, integrity, and uprightness," none of which have proven to be either his confidence or his hope. Quite the contrary. Job is mysteriously on the ash heap *because of* his fear, integrity, and uprightness. It was for these that he was chosen for the test. One might say, to paraphrase Esther: He has come to the ash heap for just such a reason as this! Thus, Eliphaz may think he is "comforting" his friend, but the effect of his words can only be exactly the opposite.

Now we may turn to the three questions I wish to raise with each of the friends (see p. 21). The first two of the questions are answered succinctly in verse 8. "Sow the wind and reap the whirlwind" (Hos. 8:7). If the harvest of one's life is sorrow, tragedy, hopelessness, and deep disturbance, the reason is obvious: That person has "plowed iniquity and sown trouble." What goes around, comes around. Eliphaz avows what common wisdom has claimed from the beginning of thought: There is a recognizable and readily describable cause and effect chain in the world of human moral action. If you do evil things, you reap evil consequences. And for Eliphaz, the source of those certain consequences for evil is no place else than God (v. 9).

Eliphaz, at this point in the story, would surely expect Job to be in full agreement. After all, in the prologue Job spent much of his time propitiating a God who was ever-ready, according to Job, to respond in fury to the slightest misstep on the part of Job's children. His continuous sacrificial gifts would surely bring a smile to the face of Eliphaz and would confirm for him what he is certain God expects from a faithful servant: obedience, awe, proper deference, and constant attention.

But Job now hears this traditional viewpoint from the far side of disaster, and the sound of it has changed. Can Job any longer really believe that an ash heap for a home is a certain sign of an evil life? And, just as importantly, can the reader of the tale any longer believe it? Has not the prologue, and Job's monologue in response to it, now cut the cord tying evil to its "inevitable" evil rewards? Yet Eliphaz is not so privileged as we. We know what he does not, namely, the certain fact that it is not evil or sin that has brought Job to his newfound lifestyle. Eliphaz may mouth the party line about the certain consequences of a life of sin, but he is completely unaware that the very one who calls the conviction into the most serious question is the one who squats before him, all-over-boils, dressed in rags, smelling of death.

In verses 12–16 Eliphaz recounts a visitation from "a spirit," an apparently heavenly being who comes to reveal to him a "wonderful" truth about life and the universe. It is a delightful description, filled with "dread" (the same word Job used to describe the horror he was anticipating from the out-of-kilter world he found himself suddenly inhabiting–3:25), "shaking bones," "hair standing up," profound "silence," and finally "a voice." It is a vision worthy of the revelation of God to Elijah on Mount Horeb in 1 Kings 19.

Unfortunately, what the spooky voice says is a distinct letdown. The verse may be read in two quite different ways.

Can a mortal be righteous before God?
Or a human pure before its maker? (v. 17)

Or:

Can a mortal be more righteous than God?
Or a human more pure than its maker? (v. 17)

If the former translation is adopted, the content of the revelation is that no human being is ever to be counted righteous or pure before God. Any claims of human righteousness are false on their face. If one tries to claim righteousness and purity, one is quite wrong.

If the latter reading is made, the revelation warns that no human should ever have the temerity to claim that he or she is more righteous and more pure than God. But, if the former reading seems hardly relevant to the story now, this reading appears less so. Job in the monologue has not claimed righteousness or purity; he has claimed disturbance and con-fusion. Whatever can Eliphaz mean by recounting his vision and its content just now?

Two answers are possible. First, the grand vision of Eliphaz has no direct relevance whatsoever! It merely adds to the portrait of the blithering buffoon that the poet intends. But another answer is that it has a kind of indirect and terrible relevance. The next two verses of the vision are indeed chilling (v. 18–19).

It is one thing to say that no human can be either righteous before God or more righteous than God. It is quite another to say that God trusts precisely no one, not even the special messengers of God. What can this mean? It appears to mean that God trusts no one to be anything other than a perpetrator of folly. Thus, the indirect and terrible relevance of the vision for Job's case is that Job is doomed to act foolishly because that is the only way a human being ever acts in the sight of God. For Eliphaz, God expects the worst from all of God's creatures. So any claims of any kind concerning right behavior or wise action are ruled out by Eliphaz' God. The dialogue, according to the theology of Eliphaz, should end now. One can imagine Eliphaz standing very erect as he recounts his vision, his eyes fixed on an unseen, far horizon. The last thing he expects from anyone is an answer to this trenchant vision that should silence all impure and foolish creatures, which categories include us all.

So now Eliphaz can be dressed. I see him tall and graying, a carefully tended beard enhancing the regal cast to his face. His deep blue robes are lavish, expensively embroidered with silver moons and golden stars and suns. He wears a tall, coni-cal hat to match. His blue-green eyes are piercing, straying often to the horizon, searching for the truth behind all things, less interested in the truth one might find closer at hand. His shoes are rich, golden brocade, the heels slightly elevated to provide just the right added height to the already imposing figure. His voice is sonorous, the deepest bass, thundering in its timbre, penetrating to the souls of his hearers. Here is a Merlin-like wizard of theology, as sure of his person as he is of the complete accuracy of his beliefs. He is supremely confident in all things, a veritable force of nature always to be reckoned with.

When Eliphaz gazed in his mirror at home before setting out on his journey to meet Job, the person described above gazed comfortably back at him. But the audience of the tale, along with Job, must see someone rather different. Job can only see a cruel and callous so-called comforter and friend. The central verse of Eliphaz' speech (4:8) to Job's ears could be nothing less than heartless. To a sufferer the implications are obvious: If those who plow evil inevitably reap it, what else could that imply except that Job is the foulest of evil-doers? Nearly every word out of Eliphaz' unctuous mouth would be heard by Job as an attack, a taunt, an unveiled attempt to proclaim that Job is a sinner.

Far from being the comforter he claims to be, and far from being the cruel discomforter that Job hears him to be, the casual reader may see him as little more than a clown, a mountebank, a puffed-up purveyor of theological banalities that are foolishly wide of the mark in the case of Job. Eliphaz bases his speech on well-worn phrases from the schools of wisdom. Indeed, verses 7–11 are little else than a series of familiar-sounding clauses.

But is Eliphaz only an unwitting fool in this first speech? I think the careful reader will conclude otherwise. The dialogue technique described in note 4 (chap. 2), namely, "being hoist on one's own petard," makes the point. The key word for Eliphaz in 4:7–11 is the word "perish." He employs the word three times in these five brief verses: 7a, 9a, 11a. It serves as a refrain for the death of the wicked. Job had used "perish" emphatically as the very first word of his speech of chapter 3: "Let the day perish in which I was born." Eliphaz picks up Job's despairing word and makes it a litany for the ultimate fate of all who are truly wicked. This can be no accident; Job's desire to die is for Eliphaz proof positive that Job is no other than a wicked person. In other words, Job's wish for death will soon be fulfilled, says Eliphaz, for so it is with all wicked persons. Again and again in subsequent speeches, Job's wish to die will be used as proof for the friends that he must be wicked, because only wicked people have such wishes.

Thus, for the careful reader of the drama, Eliphaz is not an unwitting boob at all. He is as cruel as Job hears him to be. His apparent indirect announcements concerning the fate of the wicked are in reality well-aimed arrows at his friend.

And he continues his attack in the second part of his speech, chapter 5. Two verses of the chapter are worthy of some comment (vv. 17–18). "God never gives us more than we can stand," intones the comfortable comforter. "There is a lesson in this for you, Job. God is teaching you something that you have to learn. And you can be certain that the pain will not last forever, because God is both wounder and healer, both shatterer and builder."

This notion of Eliphaz' lesson that we learn from suffering is not completely without merit. Human beings can indeed learn valuable lessons from the especially difficult trials that every life throws up. But the reader should not forget the context into which Eliphaz offers his advice. He has spent all of chapter 4 and the first part of chapter 5 denouncing Job as the foulest of sinners with words both direct and indirect. That Job has clearly brought these misfortunes down on his own head is certain for Eliphaz, who announces that the universe of God works in no other way. But now, after softening his quarry up with verbal body blows, he smiles benignly and proclaims that Job should cheer up, because God only disciplines those whom God especially loves! However helpful such advice might sound in the abstract (and I would question its helpfulness even there), the reader may only guess how heartless, how appalling the words would sound to the miserable, suffering Job. "Smile! God loves you! The proof of that love is your suffering! Of course, your suffering is at the same time the proof of your boundless evil!" Can Eliphaz finally have it both ways?

And as Eliphaz winds up his sermon to Job, his words become quite grand. He lists those things that a redeemed Job may expect from the God who has punished him out of great love but who will ultimately bring Job to safety (5:19). He will be safe from famine, war, pestilence, wild animals, and all manner of general destruction (5:20–24). Then Eliphaz, his voice resounding, his tone rotund, concludes in verses 25–26.

Verse 25 must rain down on Job like a hammer blow, for his descendants are precisely none because of the death of all of his offspring in the prologue. To Job, in a bitter irony, his offspring *are* like grass, at least as Isaiah 40:6–8 understands it; like grass, Job's offspring have been cut down and have withered. Eliphaz' peroration must seem bitter indeed to this lonely man.

An oratorical flourish ends the speech (v. 27). Eliphaz' "this" includes all the content of his speech. Job is a sinner, as are all human beings; God always gives precisely what human beings deserve; God disciplines only those God loves; and God will restore the truly penitent. Eliphaz, perhaps now speaking on behalf of his two fellow friends, says, "We have searched this out." All Job need do is to pay attention in order to know these truths as well as Eliphaz and his friends know them. I imagine the impressive wise man finishing his speech with arms outstretched, face raised to the sky in exaltation, and in anticipation of thunderous applause.

Comment

Eliphaz' opening response to the Joban monologue has been read in several different ways. He has been described as a genuinely wise counselor and comforter,[1] an unintentionally cruel ironist who had genuine comfort in mind,[2] or a directly cruel satirist whose intention is to skewer Job for his emerging impiety and his obvious longtime deeds of evil. I have argued for the third portrait, based on a careful reading of the actual words chosen by Eliphaz, words often borrowed from the Joban speech with which Job "may be hoist on his own petard." But Eliphaz' cruel intentions have rebounded on him, because he is completely unaware of what the reader knows about Job, namely, his integrity, innocence, and rejection of evil. Hence, just like a boomerang, the satiric barbs of Eliphaz return to embed themselves in his own flesh. While he thought to assail and destroy Job, he has in fact left himself open to the charge of attempted assault with a deadly weapon (i.e., his verbal test). His target is safe; it is Eliphaz himself who has received the critical wound.

We must make no mistake: Eliphaz is most certainly an evil man. Yet, his evil, as is so often true of evil, is banal, tinged with a kind of slapstick comedy. His imposing countenance, glorious voice, and superior oratory cannot ultimately hide his petty, evil purpose to obliterate the Jobs of the world, those unpleasant types who refuse to roll over in the face of the harshness of human life. Eliphaz' problem with Job may be summed up rather simply: If Job is both righteous and rejected by God, then Eliphaz' neat and clean theology is up for grabs. Eliphaz *must* destroy Job; if not, Eliphaz himself may be destroyed. He is fighting for his theological life. Thus, it is no wonder that he must employ whatever means he possesses to convert Job or to annihilate him. It is the conviction of this reading that Eliphaz has decided on the latter course. Unfortunately for him, he faces an antagonist worthy of the battle.

Job 6—7

Job wastes little time responding directly to the speech of Eliphaz in 6:2–3.

At 5:2 Eliphaz announced that "anger" will kill the fool. Job retorts that his "anger" is not gushing forth for no reason. That anger, and the calamity that engendered it, outweigh the sand of the sea. What else can he do than pour forth a flood of words in response? Eliphaz' earlier warning for Job not to be impatient when Eliphaz conducts his test of him (4:2) is mocked by Job's claim that he could act in no other way, given the volume of the horror to which he has been subjected.

In verse 4, Job says directly what he only implied in his opening speech: His problem is God. It is God who has inexplicably turned against him. Here is the central claim of Job's response to Eliphaz. He is complaining bitterly about the disasters he has suffered not only because of their devastating effects on his shattered life; even more terrible is the fact that God is the direct cause of it all. Job paints a lurid picture in this verse. God has shot poison-tipped arrows into Job's body, bringing on his weakened and shrunken appearance.

It is the inexplicability of the attack of God that most sharply differentiates Job's view of his life from Eliphaz' view of it.

Eliphaz' claim at 5:7 that "human beings are born for trouble" is denied by Job, who cries out that God has brought on Job's trouble for no reason. And rather than "be happy" for the "gift" of God's discipline, as Eliphaz enjoins at 5:17, Job is furious at the assault of God and insists that his fury is fully justified by the attack. Eliphaz has attempted to provide Job with a completely rational response to his plight, rational within the confines of Eliphaz' conceptions of the world's workings: God has acted and always knows what God is doing. Thus, happiness and acceptance must surely follow. Job is less sure that the universe in which he lives is rational and easily explicable. Thus, anger, frustration, and hopelessness may be the result. The distinctions between the two old friends are widening as the dialogue progresses.

Another sign of this widening gap can be seen in their respective understandings of hope. Twice in the speech of Eliphaz he refers to hope, at 4:6 and at 5:16. The former verse claims that those who have "integrity" have hope with God, and the latter says that because God is especially concerned with the poor and those treated unjustly, they can have hope in God. Job now responds with great bitterness to these claims at verses 8–9.

"You speak of hope, Eliphaz? You want to know what my hope is? That this strange God, who has attacked me unmercifully, without warning or reason, would go on and finish the job!" In verse 9 Job uses another word Eliphaz employed twice, the word "crush." In 4:19 Eliphaz stated that all humanity, untrusted by God, will eventually be "crushed like a moth," while in 5:4 he cruelly said that the children of fools are both "far from safety" and "crushed in the gate" without rescuer. Job now asks that this God, who seems so adept at crushing, would just do it for Job and put him out of his misery.

But the reader of the prologue might be reminded of another part of the tale by something else in verse 9. Twice in the prologue the Satan asked YHWH to "send forth his hand and touch all that he has" and "his bone and flesh" (1:11; 2:5). The result, said the Satan, would be a curse. Now Job asks that same God to "free his hand" and kill him. The God of the prologue insisted that the Satan "spare Job's life" (2:6). In the prologue such a request might have seemed generous; to Job it seems to be the worst form of cruelty. "Get it over with, God," shouts Job. This reminder of the prologue is unsettling to the reader, calling to consciousness the test of God that began the entire story. Two questions arise. Has the test failed? Job clearly wants it to end with his death. Has Job in effect cursed God? Could 6:4 be construed as a curse of God? Surely, to accuse God of sadism (poisoned arrows) and assault with attempt to maim (the arrayed terrors) must be some kind of curse, even if the word itself is not used.

Now Job rounds on the friends with direct accusations. Unfortunately, the sentence that begins his direct attack on them, and especially on Eliphaz, their first spokesman, is difficult to read.[3]

> As for those who deny kindness to a friend:
> They abandon the worship of Shaddai! (v. 14)

I translate the verse in this way for two reasons. First, it stands at the head of a very long and angry denunciation of the friends wherein Job accuses them of denying to him the most basic of human needs, namely, genuine caring for one in extreme circumstances (vv. 14–30). The word rendered "kindness" is a common and very important word in the Hebrew Bible, often used to express the unfailing devotion of God to God's people (see, for example, the extraordinary Ps. 136, where the refrain hymns the "steadfast love," or kindness, of God, seen both in history and in creation). Second, the connection between rejection of a fellow human being and true worship of God is a common one in the Bible. Proverbs 14:21 presents a clear example: "Those who despise their friends are sinners" (see also Hos. 4:1; Mic. 6:8; and the familiar 1 Jn. 4:20). Eliphaz has accused Job of being a sinner because his outward circumstances prove the case: Those who are on ash heaps after great loss are, by definition, sinners in the worldview of Eliphaz. Now Job returns the favor. Those who see a friend in need and refuse to offer care and devotion to him or her, are, by definition, people who have abandoned true worship.

Job goes on to claim that he has asked nothing from them, no gift, no bribe, no rescue, no ransom (vv. 22–23). He asks rather for enlightenment from them (vv. 24). Job has heard Eliphaz cruelly class him with the sinners, but he has yet to hear just what he has done to deserve the accusation. The verb he uses, as he asks the friends to tell him what he has done wrong, is used both in Leviticus 4 and Numbers 15 in connection with elaborate rituals designed to atone for inadvertant errors. In both cases, young bulls are to be sacrificed to cleanse the entire community for any unintentional sinning (see similarly Ezek. 45:20). There is again irony in Job's request, given his actions in the prologue. Job spent much time sacrificing for the possible sins of his children, which they may have done "in secret" (1:5). He now challenges Eliphaz and his two cohorts to reveal to him the sins he may have unknowingly committed. Job seems to want a traditional answer to his problem; if he can identify the sin, he knows well how to deal with it, having had abundant practice in response to his own children.

But there is a very significant problem with the traditional answer; there must be some sin that Job has committed that is worthy of the devastating response of God. The problem is that he cannot imagine one, nor can he discern one. So he challenges the friends to show him such a sin (vv. 28–30).

Job presents a complex challenge to his friends. I hear his first demand quite literally. The implication of the words is that the friends have physically turned their backs on Job due to the sharp rejoinders with which Eliphaz' words have been met. As is often the case with those who are completely certain of their position, they refuse to pay any attention to anyone who would dare think otherwise. Job's words have stung them, and they have no intention of giving him any more of their time.

Job demands that they pay attention to him. If they assume he is some sort of sinner, they ought at least to have the common courtesy to tell him what those sins are. He announces that he is a man of truth, and if he is shown to have done evil, however inadvertantly, he will gladly hear it, will 'fess up, and will make plans to correct the wrong. I read a familiar word in verse 29 as "integrity" in this context (it is often read "righteousness"), because Job's good name is quite obviously at stake in the debate. He has known himself to be a man of integrity, and that integrity has been challenged quite directly both by God, apparently, and by Eliphaz, certainly. Thus, Job calls for justice. If he is accused, he has the legal right to be told the reasons for the accusation. This demand for justice will again and again characterize the demands of Job. Here it is directed to the friends; soon the demand will rise up to God.

However, before that demand is sounded, at the beginning of chapter 7 Job laments the calamitous life that all human beings are forced to live. He leaves off his sharp tone of attack and somberly returns to the tone of his opening monologue (7:1–3). Of course, even in the midst of lament, Job does not miss the opportunity to use words from the speech of Eliphaz that preceded his.

An example appears in 7:3. Job refers to "nights of trouble," a word Eliphaz used twice in his first speech. Most importantly, Eliphaz announced that trouble was a certain sign of the presence of evil, because a harvest of trouble always arises from a planting of the same (4:8). Then, in a rather different belief, Eliphaz said that "human beings were born for trouble," trouble being an inescapable fact of human life (5:7). Job rejects both of these claims with the verb he employs to say how trouble has come to him. His trouble has been "appointed" for him; "set aside" or "assigned" are possible renderings. This word is carefully chosen to say clearly that Job's trouble comes neither from his supposed sin nor from the bare fact of his humanity. Quite the contrary! This trouble has been assigned to him, and from his plain accusation of 6:4, it should be clear that God is the one who has made the assignment.

While verses 1–6 of chapter 7 have a general address, verses 7ff. turn directly to God. More and more this will be the case, as Job discovers that his friends can offer him no help and that his real argument can only be with God, the cause of the disaster, as far as Job can see. In 7:7–10 Job's comments to God become remarkably and unforgettably bold and imaginative.

It is noteworthy that Job first uses an imperative verb form to call upon God to remember. This in itself is far from unique in the Hebrew Bible. God's people often remind God of things with a freedom and urgency that transcends our reticent speech with our God. Moses (Ex. 32:11–14) and many psalmists (Ps. 25:6; 74:2, 18; 89:47, 50, among others) remind God that God should remember the promises made. Job's cheeky-sounding speech is not different from many who have preceded him in Israel.

Yet he does move further toward challenge and rebuke of God when he warns God that the divine eye may at last turn toward Job, but it will then be too late. The order of the universe is that death is the end; once a person has descended to Sheol, there is no return. If God is to look upon the faithful servant and allow him once again to see good, then God had better hurry up!

And because Job's complete annihilation is near, he feels utterly free to voice his complaint in the boldest of terms. And incredibly bold he is (vv. 11–12)! In the face of certain death, Job launches his complaint filled with bitterness and anguish. Verse 12 is very important in understanding Job's basic problem. The line drips with sarcasm as Job accuses God of mistaking him for two of the monsters of chaos. Both of these creatures are well known from the Ugaritic mythological texts of the Canaanites, but even without that special knowledge, the Hebrew Bible itself contains enough references to these creatures that we can appreciate Job's point (see, for example, Isa. 51:9; Ps. 74:13–14; Gen. 1:21). These giant creatures are opposed to the activity of God and must be subdued if God's work is to be successful. And that is precisely Job's problem. Has God confused him with one of them? Is God assaulting Job because Job is seen to be some sort of cosmic threat to God's will and way?

The issue, as it has already been hinted at above, is proportionality. Job and his friends all agree at this point in the debate that the only way the universe is to be understood is through some form of the doctrine of retribution. Their differences will revolve around who is finally responsible for Job's wretched existence, Job's evil or God's inexplicable attack. For the friends it will, of course, be the former. But if Job is to accept that explanation, he will have to admit that he has done deeds so heinous as to be obvious and horrific. He cannot see any evidence of such deeds. Hence, the fault must lie with God. Surely, no peccadilloes of his youth could have brought on the avalanche of retribution evidenced by his ash heap and his broken pottery bits.

Verse 7:12 is Job's first attempt at some sort of explanation. On the face of it, the explanation appears absurd. Surely Job, in bitter sarcasm, mocks the disproportionate attack on his life by snidely snarling that God has hurled the divine terrors at the wrong creature. Perhaps God got the wrong address; Tannin must live two doors down! Yet, if it is not merely sarcasm that lies behind the phrase, the charge may be uglier still. Perhaps God is "losing it," as the modern phrase has it. Maybe God, now peering through trifocals grown too weak, has missed the proposed target. Perhaps God really has confused Job with Yam in some sort of great divine mistake? Perhaps Job is mocking the old phrase by saying, "God works in nefarious ways God's blunders to perform!" Job presents us with a terrible alternative. Either God has in fact confused Job with a primordial monster and is crushing him by mistake, or God is attacking Job on purpose and has smashed him beyond reason and beyond recognition. Neither portrait of God provides comfort for the believer.

Job then concludes his long response to Eliphaz and God with a startling series of lines (vv. 16–21). What Job says he "rejects" (NRSV "loathe") in verse 16 has been the subject of considerable discussion because the direct object that this verb ordinarily takes is not here. Perhaps it is fair to say that he rejects everything he has heard and experienced to this point along with the explanations he has received from Eliphaz to explain them. (The use of the verb "reject" without direct object occurs again at the pivotal 42:6, where its proper understanding will affect significantly the way the book is to be understood.)

Then Job's indignation at God turns to sarcasm as he twists a famous psalm into a sneering parody. Psalm 8:4 familiarly states:

What are human beings that you remember them,
mortals that you visit (inspect) them?

For the psalmist, the long memory and constant visitation of God are signs of wonder and hope for the human creature who feels so insignificant in the universe. But God's constant vigilance (the same Hebrew word can mean either "visit" for help or "search" for evil) is hardly a sign of hope for Job. Quite the contrary! Because it is this ever-present deity who has attacked and terrorized him, both directly as God's target and indirectly through the less-than-tender ministrations of Eliphaz, Job is moved to demand that God avert the divine gaze at least long enough so that he can gulp once before he dies! The ever-vigilant God has called forth rapturous praise from more than a few biblical poets (see especially Ps. 139), but if that God has become the primal enemy, as Job has determined, God's presence is little less than a terrible and unending nightmare.

The final two verses of the speech recall another series of texts, found in the book of the prophet of the exile, the so-called Second Isaiah. Here is the only other book of the Hebrew Bible in which the rare word "spit" is found (it is used once more at Job 30:10). The use is in the midst of the third servant song of Isaiah (50:6), where the mysterious servant says that he did not hide his face from "insult and spitting." Interestingly, Job uses three other words from the fourth servant song of Isaiah to conclude the speech. In Isaiah 53:4–5 the servant is said to have "carried our sorrows," to have been "bruised for our iniquities" and "crushed for our transgressions." In the mouth of Job these words become a challenge for God to play the role of the suffering servant on his behalf. If God is so intent on rooting out Job's iniquity, why doesn't God simply "carry his transgression and remove his iniquity"; would that not be a more divine thing to do than to destroy tiny Job? "Let me suggest how you might better perform the role of God," says Job, and with that amazing challenge his address ends.

Comment

Job has no intention of accepting the claims of Eliphaz, nor does he intend to take the shambles his life has become lying down. He begins the dismantling of Eliphaz' arguments by the clever use of several of Eliphaz' own words and phrases against him. Of course, the reader hardly needs to be told that Eliphaz is a cruel buffoon; she can see that for herself without the wiles of Job pointing it out. However, because Job joins the reader in her opinion of Eliphaz, Job and the reader are brought closely in line. The effect of this identity will need to be explored further as we approach the end of the tale.

Also in this speech, Job begins to discover that he can gain little satisfaction through a debate with the friends. It is God with whom he must ultimately reckon, that God who initially seemed to be on Job's side, but who now seems to have become his enemy. Just who is this Joban God? Job knows that God as one who needs and expects proper sacrifice, but who now apparently cares little for such things. This is a God who rewards the righteous and punishes the wicked, for so Job has been taught and so Eliphaz has loudly and harshly preached. But something is amiss, because Job can identify no sin that could possibly have brought on the huge losses he has experienced. So, if Job is not at fault, the only other explanation is that God is the problem. It is God who has done these terrible deeds. But why? Job and the friends are caught in a very tight box of belief. As Archibald MacLeish has it:

> I heard upon his dry dung heap
> That man cry out who cannot sleep:
> "If God is God He is not good,
> If God is good He is not God;
> Take the even, take the odd.[4]

Job and his friends are thus caught, wriggling on the sharp point of a hopeless choice between a God who does all, the good and the bad, and a God, unknown to them, who does not do all or who does only the good. It is little wonder that Job cries out in the bitterest of anguish that he will "not restrain his mouth." As we have seen, his speech has become rash, accusing God of a sadistic cruelty. Perhaps we ought not be surprised when the second friend, Bildad, weighs in to the discussion with ferocious anger and a biting sarcasm of his own.

Job 8

Bildad begins his response to Job with a straightforward warning (8:2). He uses an idiom sometimes read "how long," but the more literal translation would be "up to where." Hence, I think Bildad warns Job that he is skating on very thin ice with the kind of language he has been using. What exactly Bildad means by his general "these things" he will clarify immediately. His warning concludes with the sarcastic claim that Job's cries to God and to Eliphaz are little more than a "great wind," loud and raucous but devoid of thought and meaning, ultimately empty.

Bildad wastes little time but gets right to the point (v. 3). These rhetorical questions demand the answer, No! It is inconceivable to him that God could ever, in any way, pervert (literally, "make crooked") justice or the right. He has concluded from the lengthy speech of Job that that is precisely Job's implication. And, though Job has not said it so bluntly as this, Bildad is surely right to draw this conclusion. Job has said that God has targeted him, destroyed his life, treated him like a great monster; God in effect has perverted his right. Job will in a later speech say quite directly that God has in fact "perverted his right" (19:6), but Bildad has correctly anticipated what Job will conclude and say for himself.

On what grounds does Bildad base his argument that God certainly does not pervert anyone's right? The sheer, crass bluntness of verse 4 is breathtaking. Job's ten children got precisely what they deserved when they died in that house during one of their regular feasts. There was no perversion of justice there, because such cataclysmic events are hardly uncaused. Evil was being done somewhere, says Bildad, and evil was appropriately and swiftly and thoroughly punished. Job himself had feared as much; that is why his sacrifices were so numerous and so frequent. Bildad merely says that Job's worst fears were realized in fact. Still, the reader is stunned by the directness of Bildad's statement about Job's dead children. If he imagines this to be comfort (2:11) of some sort, it must appear to Job, and to any slightly sensitive reader, to be cold comfort at best. This sentence is the very stuff of hostility, because Bildad senses rightly what Job's rantings imply: There is the very deepest of challenges to the worldview of the friends locked up in Job's words. This is no time for politeness and charm! They really are engaged with "principalities and powers"; how else could they evaluate Job's claims against God, given their theological beliefs?

After Bildad's swift and decisive rejection of Job's nonsense about an unjust God, he offers to Job the answer to all of his problems (vv. 5–7). These three verses nicely summarize Bildad's prescription for Job's ultimate success. The process Job must follow to extricate himself from his home among the ashes is twofold. First, he must "eagerly seek" God. This verb is built on the word for "dawn" and suggests urgency in the activity of searching for something. Bildad is responding directly to Job's challenge to God in 7:21 that God will one day "eagerly seek" (from the same verbal root) him, but it will be too late, for Job will be dead. By employing this same word, Bildad accuses Job of a dangerous delusion: It is not God who will desperately search for good old Job. On the contrary! It is Job who must desperately seek God, if his life is to be turned in the right direction. In the second line of verse 5 Bildad urges Job to "implore the favor of" God. The classical place wherein this form of the verb is used is 1 Kings 8, where three times Solomon, while blessing the temple in Jerusalem, urges all of Israel to "implore the favor of" God (vv. 33, 47, 59). And in 1 Kings 9:3, God responds favorably to the people's "imploring," using the same form. Thus, Bildad peppers his sermon to Job both with Job's own words, in the poet's usual style, and with famous illustrations from Israel's fabled past, all with one intent: to convert Job to Bildad's way of thinking.

But Job's eager seeking and earnest imploring are merely step one on the road to transformation. As Job seeks God, he must be certain that he is both "pure" (*zak*) and "upright" (*yashar*). This certainty is step two, although it is a step that must be taken simultaneously with the other if success is to be achieved. About the latter word the reader has no doubt, because the prologue has used it three times with reference to Job (1:1, 8; 2:3), and Eliphaz employed the word in a vain attempt to convince Job that those who were "upright" were never cut off (4:7). Job, the upright one, has in fact been cut off.

Bildad's other word, "pure," represents its first use in the poem, but by no means its last. Zophar will use the word in his first speech, as will Eliphaz in his second. Job, too, will not

miss the chance to speak the word in a later speech. This word
is an ethical term most frequently used in wisdom contexts (cf.
Prov. 20:9; Ps. 51:7; 73:13; 119:9). Bildad connects it to the
word "upright," perhaps to emphasize the strict requirements
of moral purity one must have to approach God without fear
and with any hope to be restored.

If Job is purely upright, and if he eagerly and earnestly
implores the favor of the Almighty One, he can be assured
that God will rise up in his behalf, restore Job to his proper
righteous place, and bless him with a future marked by great
abundance. It is an evangelical sermon worthy of a Billy Sunday, and Bildad expects nothing less from Job than a heartfelt
admission of his obvious evil and a tearful return to God down
the Shuhite equivalent of the sawdust trail.

Now, as with Eliphaz, we want to ask of Bildad the question of the origin of the theology that undergirds his sermon to
Job. His answer is clear, offered in verses 8–10.

All important answers are to be found in the past. Bildad
is, in effect, a Shuhite church historian. No human being can
be trusted to have the fund of knowledge necessary to live life
successfully, because our spans of life are too brief, no more
than a shadow. Hence, says Bildad, we must attend to the
founders, those first and greatest thinkers of our race, who left
us with crucial guidance wherewith we may maneuver through
the minefields of life. Such advice is sound and needs a continuous sounding.

But what exactly is Job to learn from Bildad's history lesson? Verses 11–22 provide the answer, an answer that sounds
all too familiar to Job and to us. Bildad begins the lesson with a
proverb that announces universal truth (v. 11). The answer to
these rhetorical questions is obviously, No. But the real point
of remembering these bits of truth from the world of plants is
made clear by verses 12–13.

Without water the papyrus withers; without God all hope
is gone. The sermon seems clear enough, but the second line
of verse 13 deserves a closer look.

The two words "hope" and "perish" should be familiar to
the reader by now. Eliphaz said at 4:6 that the "integrity of
one's ways" should be one's "hope." The implication was that

because Job in his opening monologue clearly demonstrated little hope, he certainly could not be a man of integrity. Job had retorted in 7:6, punning on the dual meaning of the word (it means both "hope" and "thread"), that his hope was fast-disappearing just like the thread flying through a weaver's shuttle. Now Bildad warns that all who forget God can have no hope. The fact that Job has said that he has no hope is for Bildad proof positive that he has in fact forgotten God; only those without God would ever say that they are without hope! For Bildad, Job has skewered himself on his own words. Or perhaps better said, Bildad thinks he has skewered Job with Job's own words.

Bildad closes his first address with a summary of his sermon to Job (vv. 20–22). One can imagine Bildad ending his speech with energy and drama, matching the sweeping rhetoric of his words. Because he has the certainty of long-hallowed tradition on his side, he anticipates no contradiction to his forceful words. If Job closely follows the advice of verses 5–7, advice that is the certain conclusion of the ancient wisdom of verses 11–19, the result will be joy and laughter, coupled with the outright humiliation and eventual annihilation of all of Job's enemies. Bildad has spoken neatly and crisply, using an admirably brief selection of words. He surely sits with a satisfied smile of triumph, fully expecting Job to approach the mourner's bench with appropriate contrition.

It is important to remember at this stage of the drama that the three characters who have spoken so far all agree on one very important fact: God has directly brought suffering to Job. Where they disagree is in their explanations concerning why God has done so. "Discipline!" shouts Eliphaz. "Punishment!" shouts Bildad. "Divine mistake!" or "Divine maliciousness!" or "Divine stupidity!" shouts Job. The interlocutors agree on page one of the tale, but thoroughly disagree about the unfolding plot in which they find themselves.

And now we may clothe the second friend. Because he is a teacher, steeped in the lore of wisdom, Bildad is dressed in academic black, three prominent chevrons on each sleeve, indicating his advanced degrees in theology. On his head is the classic mortarboard, doctoral tassle dangling jauntily. His steel-rimmed glasses are round and very thick, the result of too many late nights reading dusty tomes under bad lighting. His back is bowed slightly from the seated, hunched posture of the scholar. His graying hair pokes out from under his mortarboard at crazy angles; Bildad is far too busy to lower himself to mundane acts like hair-combing. His shoes are unshined, old, the heels worn down from walking from important seminar to important lecture. His voice is high pitched, somewhat raspy from hard use in the fray of argument and the demands of the lecture hall filled with large classes. His eyes are blue-green, piercing but shifting quickly from face to face, from ground to sky. His satchel bulges with books, some old with flecks of binding spotting the inside of the satchel, while some are new, bearing Bildad's own name on their colorful covers. Here is the scholar par excellence, a creature of the mind, a man of the library and the study, sure of his knowledge, ever ready to engage another mind in spirited debate. Yet, because he is a teacher of theology, there is much of the preacher in him, too, not willing simply to impart information, but anxious to say it in such a way as to persuade, to cajole, finally to convert. Bildad is no impartial scholar. He is a militant evangelist, and all of his great learning is put to the task of proclaiming the truth, a truth that brooks little or no contradiction.

Comment

As always, we need to take stock as we proceed through the tale. It is far too easy as one reads Job to lose the forest for the trees. What has Bildad added to the tale? If Eliphaz is a cruel buffoon, then Bildad is equally cruel, if perhaps not so clownish as his friend. Bildad weighs in directly with his astonishing jibe of verse 4 that God killed Job's children in the prologue for the perfectly understandable reason that they had committed some egregious sins. There is less nonsense to Bildad, less subtlety, far less beating-around-the-bush than we saw in Eliphaz. The world is exactly like this, and is to be seen in no other way; God's activities are all equally clear and understandable. Just as certainly as papyrus needs water, so do evil folk get precisely what they deserve from a God who is as reliable in action as the world of nature. All Job needs to do is to seek God and to submit to God's certain control of all things and events. The result will be restored joy and laughter.

But unlike Bildad, neither Job nor the reader is sanguine about the world and the activity of God in it. Too often, the poet reminds us of the words of the prologue and subsequent speeches that are profoundly troubling. Those key words include: "blameless," "upright," "evil," "perish," among others that will play roles in the ensuing drama. We readers know too much about Job, far more than his friends know, to accept so readily their cookie-cutter views of God and God's way with the world. They are very quick to summarize, very eager to generalize, extremely unwilling to listen to any evidence that might deflect them from their hardened truths, learned from revelation and from the trustworthy traditions of the past. They have placed Job in his appropriate box: sinner. What he must do is admit whatever evil he has done in order to be readmitted into their world, the ordered world designed and sustained by God by means of readily accessible laws.

However, if Bildad, very like his fellow friend Eliphaz, thinks that Job is now ready to accede to their superior wisdom, is anxious to wail out his sins to the mercy seat of heaven, he is about to be most rudely disappointed. Far from being ready to admit his guilt and their knowledge, Job is driven to ever-harsher comments about them and about the God they claim to represent.

Job 9—10

Chapter 9 is a key chapter for the dialogue and for our understanding of the entire book. Job's accusations against God reach a pitch nearly unmatched in the remainder of his speeches, and, as always, he uses the words of his friends to make these accusations. The crass bluntness of the friends in their attempts to skewer Job as evil, far from bringing about his repentance, have rather driven him to greater flights of rage against them and against God.

Job begins his third speech with what sounds like a curt dismissal of the thoughts of his two friends. When he asks, "But how can a mortal be righteous with God?" he raises a question that he will pursue in the remainder of this chapter. But what exactly does he mean by the question? Obviously, he makes some reference to Eliphaz' question (4:17).

For Eliphaz, the answer was that any mortal claims to righteousness were to be rejected out of hand. After all, God trusted no one, not even angels, so righteousness before God was plainly impossible.

But Job is not so certain. Note how he asks the question: "*How* can a mortal be righteous *with* God?" The implication is that there may be some way to do it. Asking the question in this way directly contradicts Eliphaz' vision from on high. However, it does not necessarily deny the righteousness of God, which might best be understood as God's ability and willingness to make a person right. Eliphaz apparently fears a human arrogance that could threaten the final authority of the Divine One. Job asks whether the Divine One really does listen to the cries and the suffering of God's creatures and would be willing to discuss God's ways with them. Job wants to talk with God; he wants to know if such a thing is even possible. That is why he uses "with" instead of Eliphaz' "before." Job seeks genuine divine conversation. He is no longer satisfied with what he has been taught, no longer willing to accept the ideas employed by Eliphaz and Bildad.

Such a desire sounds pleasant enough in the abstract, but immediately Job is confronted again by what he has long believed about the God with whom he would converse (vv. 3–4). Job is forced to remember that it is God, no less, whom he desires for a dialogue partner. But Job reveals much about his understanding of this God by his choice of words. He employs four verbs (plus an auxiliary one) in these two verses, and each of them has a decidedly confrontational tone. Job, in fact, does not envision a dialogue with God, but a debate. The word I have translated "dispute" has long connections with the law courts of Israel. Especially in the prophets it is said that God has a "lawsuit" with God's sinful people (see, for example, Isa. 3:13; Mic. 6:1–2; Jer. 12:1). In this scenario God is both accuser and judge, while Israel is the plaintif. Job sees himself in the role of accuser, with God in the dock answering Job's wiley questions.

But in the second line of verse 3 the hoped-for portrait changes. Job does not now see himself as the accuser, but the accused, at whom God would direct a barrage of questions, not one of which Job could hope to answer. What has the record of such confrontations with the all-wise and all-powerful diety been? The answer is that no one has ever won a debate with God. Or, if the second line of verse 4 is translated rather differently, no one who has ever "resisted" God has "survived" (the familiar *shalom*, albeit an unusual form). In either case Job sees no real hope in a verbal struggle with God.

What does this hopeless portrait of a foolish court battle tell us about Job's understanding of God? Job's God is completely dominant, thoroughly unyielding, unwilling to listen to any mortal who would dare to confront the divine power or to call it into question. In short, Job's God is the God of the friends, most especially the God of Eliphaz! Or so it seems at the end of verse 4. But the remarkable hymn that follows (vv. 5–10) paints a far darker and more dangerous picture than we have seen to this point.

Job cannot confront God, nor will God listen to Job, because God is a deity bent on displays of unimaginable power, a power not always used for creation's good. Sometimes God's rage is so terrifying and uncontrollable that God moves the very mountains themselves before they are aware (v. 5). Then, God brings an earthquake (v. 6). Job concludes his hymn at verse 10 with a near-direct quote from Eliphaz, who began his own hymn to God with these two phrases at 5:9. The fact that Job quotes his friend almost word for word draws the reader's attention to a comparison of the two hymns.

Eliphaz employs his hymn to buttress his call to Job to "seek El," the God who does "great things" and "astonishing deeds." Eliphaz goes on to describe just what those deeds are in 5:10–16. God's deeds, according to Eliphaz, are nearly all actions directed toward human beings. After one example from nature (rain, v. 10), Eliphaz hymns God's "raising up the lowly," "lifting mourners to safety," "frustrating the crafty," "saving the needy," "offering hope to the poor." One sees God's deeds by witnessing how God acts in the lives of mortals.

Yet, for Job, that is precisely what he does *not* see. His own life and experience are constant testimony that Eliphaz' claims are nonsense. Job sees God most readily in the terrors and horrors of a violent and unpredictable nature. And because God is so overwhelmingly powerful, Job cannot meet God in order to discuss the apparent cracks that have formed in the universe. If the great monsters who tried in vain to stop the world's creation were forced in the end to worship the creator God, how in the world could tiny Job gain an audience with God? This absurd disparity of power leads Job to despair. Any confrontation with God would in fact be no genuine dialogue at all. God would not listen, being intent on crushing, wounding, and gouging Job with bitterness.

Following these accusations that God is some sort of hearing-impaired tyrant, Job is led to make what may be the most repugnant claims about the nature of God in the entire Bible (vv. 21–24). In contrast to Eliphaz, who asserted God's indifference, Job indicts God with an active immorality, the perverse desire to destroy both good and bad folk indiscriminately, accompanied by the scornful joy of watching their death throes.

Job's plight indeed appears to be hopeless. Though he is blameless, and at the same time is being treated as if he were not, he has no chance of finding justice for his cause, because the very one who is destroying him is the final arbiter of whatever justice there may be! Nevertheless, Job has a burst of hopeful imagination later in this speech (vv. 32–33; cf. 16:18–22 and 19:23–27).

Job presents this imaginative cry for a mediator precisely when such a thing seems quite ludicrous. Job's initial cries for death and disappearance from the pages of history are not what he finally demands. His ultimate demand will be for justice after a confrontation with God, the supposed source of such justice. Job is growing before our eyes, enlarging his understanding of the universe and his proper place in it. No longer is he the whining and aggrieved one who wishes he were dead or had never been. Job's friends have goaded him away from his desire for the ultimate rest of Sheol (chap. 3) to the recognition that his cries have merit (chap. 6) and now to the amazing characterization of God as divine beast (chap. 9). They wanted Job to change, all right, but much to their horror they have created a "monster" who has no intention of repenting or of going quietly into that good night.

Chapter 10 continues Job's sharp attacks on the injustice and horror of his situation (vv. 1–3). When Job says that he loathes his life, he appears to mean that he feels free to say anything he wishes about God and the universe. But what else can Job do but continue to try to attract God's attention, to engage God in discussion, to force God to answer the charges Job hurls at heaven?

So, Job can cry, "Don't condemn me!" There are no grounds on which Job should be found guilty of any misdeed worthy of these atrocities. In verse 3, he becomes more personal with God, moving from the nonexistent reasons for God's attacks to the personal reasons why God has chosen to make the attacks. Is there something in this for God? Should God be acting this way? Does God take pleasure in it? Does it improve God's reputation? Any or all of these possibilities share in the portrait of a God gone wild, a deity out of control.

Job next appeals to God's past acts of creating and sustaining Job's life (vv. 8–12). God apparently took such time and care with Job's formation that it seems inconceivable that God now would swallow that life whole, translate it so rudely back to the dust from which it came. "Remember," says Job, employing a favorite tactic of the psalmists to urge God's saving actions in times of trouble. But before God can say or do a thing by way of response to this characteristic cry of lament, Job snarls a different tune of God's real actions (vv. 13–15).

God's supposed care and love for creation were nothing but a sham. While God was apparently creating human beings with care and imbuing them with divine devotion, hidden deep in the recesses of God's devious heart was the real reason for the entire charade. "These things" and "this," cruelly vague designations for the shambles of Job's life, designed by the evil

God of creation, were and are God's intentions for the world God has made. The "care" with which God supposedly "guarded" (*shamar*) Job's spirit (v. 12) was in reality the ever-vigilant "guard" (*shamar*) of God (v. 14), hungrily snooping for Job's next sin.

Is it any wonder in the light of these beliefs about God that Job closes his third speech with a veritable lexicon of words for gloom (vv. 20–22)? His only hope in this universe gone sour, mismanaged by a monstrous or foolish deity, is a quick exit from it to a place of darkness, the land of death, "where light is darkness." In this life all one can hope for is for God to "let me alone that I may brighten a little" (v. 20). The irony for Job is that with God the world is a dark place, and without God, in death, it is also a dark place. But better darkness without this God than a world of darkness ruled by this God.

Comment

Chapters 9–10 are important for the overall design of the story of Job in several ways.

1. Job clearly and directly announces his basic beliefs about God, beliefs from which he never deviates until God's appearance. God is a monster, a beast, a sadist, unconcerned with human goodness or evil, raw in power, brutal in behavior.
2. Job demands a confrontation with this God but says that if such a thing ever happened, God would not listen, but would ask a myriad of unanswerable questions out of a hurricane of wind and storm (9:16–18). When we reach the end of the book and witness the appearance of God, these Joban words will need to be remembered.
3. Job boldly proclaims his innocence (9:20–21). In saying this he does not imply that he has never sinned. On occasion, he admits to certain sins. But whatever sins he may have committed can in no way be seen as the trigger for the absurd overkill of the attacks of God. Whatever has happened to Job cannot be commensurate with any sins he may have committed. Job's ruined life is not a sign that he has sinned. God is wrong; there can be no other explanation.

4. Job refers here for the first time to some supposed third party in the drama, pitting God against Job. In 9:33 Job names this figure an umpire or mediator and imagines that this figure might come to equalize the contest by taking God's wrath and power away long enough for Job and God to have a real discussion. However, Job quickly rejects the possibility of such a figure and concludes the speech with his only real hope of a dark death (10:20–22). But this idea of a third figure will appear again prominently in the story.

One could almost expect the dialogue to end in chapter 10. Job has come to believe that there is no escape from this uncaring, even sadistic, deity save death. His two friends have offered nothing but pious platitudes in the face of Job's enormous tragedy; their words have been cruel and callous. Job has nowhere to turn. Death is apparently his only true friend and hope. But the dialogue is far from over. I suggest that, ironically, Zophar reenergizes the discussion by the very meanness and unforgettable monstrousness of his response to the dialogue he has heard. Job will not let Zophar's words go unchallenged any more than Zophar can let Job's words go without bold comment. The dialogue must continue, for the hatred and fear of the friends for Job has not run its course, nor has Job's ultimate demand for a confrontation with God been realized.

Job 11

Zophar's anger is palpable as he enters the debate. He has had ample time to consider his response to Job, having listened to the views of his friends and Job's attacks on them as "treacherous torrent-beds" (6:15). More seriously, Zophar has heard Job talk about God in ways that are horrifying to him. God is a beast, a monster, a fool, confused and unjust. It is no wonder that Zophar is ready to burst with righteous indignation at this foul blasphemer (vv. 2–3).

Zophar's opening suggests that he has found the answers of his two friends to Job to be negligible. Verse 2 is directed as much or more to those friends as it is to Job. Zophar characterizes Job and his speeches with three degrading words or phrases:

"mass of words" (literally, "multitude of words"), "lippy man" (literally, "man of lips"–our modern slang "lippy" gets at his meaning rather nicely), and "chatter" (sometimes "babble" or "idle talk"). Job's speeches are just a mad rush of words and can easily be refuted. And Zophar is precisely the one who will refute Job, or as he says, to "humiliate" him.

Zophar has very specific accusations to make concerning what he thinks Job has said about himself and about God. He is the first of the friends to be quite so specific, and it is this specificity that will especially energize Job to his sharpest rejoinder (vv. 4–6). Unfortunately, Zophar's specific accusations are not as clear as we might like them to be. He first claims that Job said that his "doctrine is pure." What Zophar means by his use is, more generally, Job's claims, his basic beliefs. If that is his meaning, one can see why Zophar could only scoff at Job's belief that such appalling claims are "pure." The very farthest thing from the truth is that Job's doctrine is pure in any sense of the word, according to Zophar.

Zophar has also heard Job say that he is "clean" in the sight of God. But has Job in fact said that he is either "clean" or "pure"? His later claim that his "prayer is pure" (16:17) is hardly the same thing as claiming that he is pure. Has Zophar projected onto Job some concerns that especially trouble him, about the purity of doctrine and the cleanliness of human beings before God? Whatever his confusion, Zophar will offer answers to questions and problems, whether or not Job has raised them!

Zophar concludes his initial rejection of Job's claims by stating that God has made Job forget part of his evil. In other words, there are such depths of depravity in Job that God has made Job forget. Zophar knows that Job has in fact done terrible things; his position on the ash heap makes that clear enough. And Job would know it, too, if God would unveil his mind so that he could remember. But, of course, that is the problem. Job can never know the depths of his own evil. But just how does Zophar know that (vv. 7–9)?

Zophar now begins his refutation of the twin claims that Job's doctrine is pure and that he is clean in the sight of God by saying his answers are hidden in the infinite limits of the Almighty! Job, like all humans, is not privy to any such speculation.

Of course, by the logic of such an argument Zophar can hardly know anything either, but that fact does not prevent him from going on to tell Job what he thinks he, Zophar, knows (vv. 11–12).

Verse 12 is one of the poet's wonderful "one-liners." Only here in the Hebrew Bible is the word "hollow" used metaphorically. Job, the most hollow man Zophar knows, will gain understanding on the same day that the colt of a wild donkey is born human. A delightful and memorable way to say, Never!

But from where does Zophar's prodigious knowledge of God come? While Eliphaz has his vision and Bildad relies on the written and spoken lore of the ages, Zophar simply knows one thing: All wisdom and knowledge are with God alone, and folks like Job have no possible access to such knowledge. Zophar, on the other hand, simply knows what he knows and does not need visions or a lifetime of study to prove it to himself or to anyone else. "If only God would speak," he says, "and tell you the mysteries of wisdom." The implication is that God has in fact spoken to Zophar the mysteries of wisdom and has deputized him to relay the mysteries to the world. But when faced with the raucous Job, it is all the wise Zophar can do to restrain his fury in order to speak the mysteries he has been called to speak.

For persons like Zophar, it is quite irrelevant which questions are being asked, because the answers to all questions are the same: God knows and you don't. Whether Zophar quite understands Job's basic concerns is unimportant. What is important to Zophar is that he has had his indisputable say. He, like his two friends who preceded him, fully expects a repentant Job to join him at the altar to be received back into the good graces of the wonderfully forgiving God.

Now we should dress our third friend. I see him in a fine suit of excellent cloth, covering a superb white silk shirt, crowned with a tasteful tie. His shoes are Italian leather. A fresh carnation is in his buttonhole; a handkerchief, neatly matching the thread of the suit, protrudes daintily from his coat pocket. He carries a beautifully bound book, its pages well-thumbed, its edges gilt. His voice is high-pitched but not unpleasant, the slightest bit of nasalness creeping in when certain vowels are uttered at high volume. He is a practiced orator, but not a seasoned debater. He is used to having the final say in discussions and tends to repeat phrases and words he has learned well through a lifetime of public speaking. He is slightly overweight—too many fine dinners in fine restaurants during revivals and preaching missions—but the superb cut of his tailored clothes hides the expanding paunch well. Above all, he is confident, supremely confident, that his word is unimpeachable, his speech unanswerable, his sermon not to be improved. No one is more surprised than Zophar when Job not only answers him, but does so with energy and vehemence.

Comment

Zophar's first speech is, on the surface, the first genuine extended attempt to respond directly to the claims of Job. He has heard Job say that his "doctrine is pure" and his life "clean." Zophar rejects both claims with his counterclaim that God is the only one who can make such judgments, but the content of those judgments is locked deeply into the mysteries of God. Unfortunately, Zophar seems to have misheard what Job is saying. Job has not claimed that he is always clean and pure in life and thought. He merely wants to know what those sins might be that he has supposedly committed that would have led God to assault him so abominably. No one has yet offered any listing of such sins. The friends will eventually provide such a list (see Eliphaz' final speech in chap. 22), but only after Job's stubbornness has driven them to desperate words.

Again, the reader must not forget that Job and the friends agree at a very basic level about the reasons for God's actions in the world: God does reward the righteous, and God does punish the wicked. Job believes that every bit as much as the friends do; his extraordinary concern for correct and lavish sacrifice in the prologue is based on that belief. If Job did not believe that, he would not continue his demands that God act in the way Job has always believed God should act. The basic problem for Job is that, as far as his experience reveals it to him, God has stopped acting in this long-hallowed way. As for the friends, it is crucial that they convince Job of his certain evil in order that the basic belief of God's rational action can be reaffirmed. It must be Job who is evil; the alternative is unthinkable and unimaginable. Zophar goes to extreme verbal lengths to put the horns of evil squarely on Job's scabrous head, and the harsh rhetorical flourish with which he ends his sermon about the fate of the wicked makes it clear that he thinks his riposte has won the day. One can picture him, and Eliphaz and Bildad, now standing expectantly, smiles of satisfaction creasing their faces, awaiting the confession of Job that they have been right all along.

Job 12—14

Job concludes the first cycle of speeches with his longest address to date. Its seventy-five verses include direct rejoinders to the friends as well as some especially pungent retorts to God. I believe that it was the pointed attacks on Job from the mouth of Zophar (however beside the point those attacks were) that led directly to this energetic speech. Job's wish to go quickly to the gloomy land of death at the end of chapter 10 is replaced here with lively rejections of the assertions of the friends and equally lively accusations of God's continual misuse of divine power.

Job goes right after the central claim of the friends, their supposed superior wisdom (vv. 2–3). Each of them in his own way has drawn upon unique wisdom to attempt to prove Job to be a sinner. In one sarcastic phrase Job tells the three what he thinks of their wisdom (v. 2) and then states flatly, "I have a mind like you have." Job has been stung by that memorable phrase from Zophar in 11:12. Job gives sarcasm for cruelty and adds that he is in no way inferior to these three buffoons, particularly when it comes to questions of knowledge. Job, too, has knowledge, and his knowledge is more than equal in quality to that of the friends.

To understand the force of Job's argument as the speech continues, it is necessary to appreciate what he means in the last line of verse 3. "Who does not know things like these" literally says, "With whom are not things like these?" We have said all along that Job and the friends continue to have large areas of agreement among them. Job and the friends agree that God can do all things. Job and the friends agree that God is supposed to reward the righteous and punish the wicked. Job and the friends agree that God is responsible for all acts under heaven. Indeed, who does not know things like these?

Verses 4–6 demonstrate what can only be called a crack in the cosmos. First, Job says he is a "just, blameless man." He uses familiar and important words here. He is *tsaddik tamim.* The texts of the Hebrew scriptures are riddled with references to righteous ones, so-called because they have found the special favor of God (see Gen. 6:9; 18:17–19; Ps. 1; 5; 7; 10; and a host of others). Job's terrible experience is an argument against this long-held belief that God takes special care of the righteous. To the contrary, says Job. I, the righteous one, am now a joke, a laughingstock. Bildad promised that God would "fill his mouth with laughter" (8:21), but the only laughter Job hears is that of those friends who laugh uproariously at him. If righteous ones can become the butt of cruel jokes, the world is out of joint.

Second, in verse 5,[5] not only does the righteous Job find himself the object of scornful humor, there is in his world a general attitude of "derision for calamity," rather than sympathy for those in trouble. Job also says that the disabled, rather than helped as they stumble on injured feet, are attacked with a cruel cynicism. This pathetic portrait of a callous society adds to the sum of Job's knowledge of the world, a world quite different from the one painted by the friends.

Third, and perhaps most terrible of all, is the fact that God does nothing about this world gone bad. Brutality is the order of this world; might makes right. The reading of the NRSV, "the tents of robbers," is not strong enough. The "destroyers" of verse 6 are not simple petty thieves; they are monstrous and formidable foes who intend mayhem in the world. By so intending, they "provoke El," who remains strangely silent. And rather than being held by the power of God, the Almighty, they attempt by their own power to hold God! They fancy themselves the real power of the world; God becomes someone they control.

"These things," says Job, are crucial for the friends to add to their so-called wisdom. The world is a brutal place, a world predictable and settled and secure. Destroyers are safe and

active, the righteous are objects of derision, and God cares
not a fig.

And then, in a kind of parody of the friends' attempts to
convince Job of their wisdom by telling him the sources of that
wisdom, Job now tells them where he discovered the cruel wisdom he has just shared (vv. 7–10). "The heavens are telling the
glory of God," begins Psalm 19, but for Job what the creation
tells about God is the simple fact that God has done *this*. "This"
can only be the description of the world just given by Job in
verses 4–6, a world of cruelty and derision, destruction and
hatred. Job hymns the cruel side of God, the side his life experience has shown him. This, too, he says, is wisdom.

Verses 13–25 constitute Job's cruel hymn. We can best understand this hymn as a harsh parody of Psalm 107. That psalm
announces its concern for thanksgiving, for deliverance by God
in the first verse and throughout its seven scenes. "O, give thanks
to YHWH, who is good: because God's steadfast love endures
forever." In verses 8, 15, 21, 31, and 43, the words "steadfast
love" appear as a litany, calling the psalmist to respond to the
incalculable actions of God's deliverance. But Job's hymn moves
in murkier waters.

He affirms, as always, that God has unimaginable power,
and that power is wedded to a kind of divine wisdom (v. 13).
The four nouns of the verse are traditional descriptors of the
wonders of the divine one. The reader now anticipates a traditional hymn to the power, wisdom, and plan of God who di-
rects these superb skills to the benefit of God's beloved
creatures. But Job never moves in traditional ways.

A list of the verbs Job uses to portray the actions of God in
the hymn will make the point. God, says Job, "tears down,"
"shuts in," "withholds" the water to cause drought, "lets loose"
the water to cause floods, "leads counselors away naked,"
"makes fools of kings," "looses the belts of kings" (i.e., reveals
their nakedness), "replaces their belts of honor with poor loin-
cloths," "leads priests away naked," "destroys the powerful,"
"makes mute," "makes addled," "pours contempt," "makes
nations great, then destroys," "makes nations huge, then makes
them disappear," "strips the will," "makes people stagger like

drunkards." It is an astonishing list of the brutal actions of a God of supposed wisdom and understanding!

In verse 16 most specifically Job parodies the hope of Psalm 107. That psalmist gave thanks to the God who "pours contempt on princes" (Ps. 107:40), that is, princes who have "oppressed and troubled" (v. 39) the "hungry" (v. 36) and the "needy" (v. 41). For the psalmist, this God is on the side of the poor against the depredations of the powerful. Job agrees that "God pours contempt on princes" (12:21, the identical phrase), but it is not because God is acting for the oppressed. Because both "deceived and deceiver" are in God's ruthless power, all persons receive from God the same thing, namely, the back of God's hand, rather than the gift of the power of that hand to save them from trouble.

In the second part of this long speech Job says to the friends that his real dialogue partner must be God. "But I will speak to Shaddai; I will argue with God!" We might expect now to hear more of what we have already heard: the nature of God's monstrousness, the fact of God's injustice, and so on. But Job now turns on the friends in uncontrolled fury (vv. 4–5). This concerted attack on his long-winded companions is worthy of some comment. Job knows he must deal with the real source of his problems, God, but for now he feels it is time to put these loudmouths in their appropriate places. He begins by calling them "plasterers of lies" and "worthless physicians." The former figure is dependent on the word's use in one of the prophet Ezekiel's imaginative, allegorical pictures of false prophets. (Ezek. 13:10–11; Job's word "plaster" is often translated in Ezekiel as "whitewash.")

In short, Job says that his friends are trying to put a false face on the real truth of things. To put it more directly, they simply will not listen to Job's experiences. They cannot listen precisely because those experiences are not compatible with their theological platitudes.

And Job goes on to accuse these would-be healers of being in fact "worthless physicians." By employing this particular word, Job connects the so-called healing ministrations of the friends to their opposite. They are not healing Job with their words; they are rather wounding him and killing him with their lies. Finally, he tells them just to "shut up," because in their silence they will find true wisdom. The friends have spoken often to Job about his need for the wisdom of God and his own obvious lack of wisdom. Job's retort is that their babblings against him are so far from wisdom as to be worthless and cruel. Their best bet is silence.

But Job has more than an attack on the friends in mind in this speech. He also wishes to issue them a stern warning that their attacks on him are leading them into very dangerous waters with God (vv. 9–12). He warns them that God's examination can be terrible; they should not so blithely speak for God. Their day of testing might one day come, as it has for Job.

Job concludes this second part of his fourth speech in two ways. First, he challenges the friends again to be silent while he courageously confronts God with his legal case (vv. 13–14). He will do this even though death at God's hands is well-nigh certain; that is clearly the upshot of the disputed verse 15. "Yes, he will kill me: I have no hope! Nevertheless, I will defend my ways right in his face!" (This reading is of course far different from the KJV's "Though he slay me, yet will I trust in him: but I will maintain mine own ways before him.") The translation turns on matters of grammar, syntax, and theology. The KJV is barely defensible even grammatically and assumes certain textual changes. Both contextually and grammatically, my reading seems the correct one.[6]

The second way in which Job concludes is to turn back to God in the attempt to force God to confront him. He asks two things of God (v. 20). God must "withdraw God's hand," and God must not allow God's "dread" to "terrify" Job. This was precisely Job's vain hope in 9:34b, employing the same words. Job has returned to his hope for a mediator that he had earlier abandoned. He asks for no intermediary here, but calls to God directly to remove God's hand and God's dread from Job so that the court case may proceed. Then Job launches right in to the central concern of his case (v. 23).

Job still believes in the old saw that the good are rewarded and the wicked punished. Hence, if he could simply be shown wherein he has erred to bring about such grotesque punishment, he will be happy to cede the case to God. Yet the reader now gets the strong feeling that Job simply does not believe that God can come up with any sort of list of Joban sins. This is made more certain when the next verse accuses God of hiding (v. 24). From some far-off, hidden heaven, the great God of the universe spends divine time by scaring leaves and chasing worthless chaff (v. 25). Instead of meeting Job in court God is wasting time in trivial affairs of absolutely no consequence. Yet Job carries God's indictment that consists of Job's complete destruction and abasement for nothing more than the minor sins of his youth. Does God destroy Job's cattle for a schoolyard lie? Does God obliterate Job's house for Job's theft of penny candy from the local store? Surely, the Creator of the heavens and the earth can do better than that!

But apparently not, for Job ends this speech, and the first cycle of speeches, with a grim and bitter portrait of the harsh life of humanity lived in a universe ruled by an uninterested and uncaring God (14:1–2). These haunting words seem to embody only pathos and bitterness. However, we have seen more in Job than this in the earlier parts of this speech. His energy was high in chapter 12 as he scornfully rejected the deadening advice of the friends, and that energy continued in chapter 13 as he confronted them directly with their own lies and dangerous attempts to plead the case for God. Has he returned to the more melancholy mood of his earlier speeeches?

I think the answer is no. The fuller context of this speech cannot allow us to limit Job to melancholy alone (vv. 3–6). Job here states the fact of the brevity of human life and then demands that the author of that pathetic life, God, get away from us long enough for us to experience at least the joy available to a hired hand, as minimal and fleeting as that might be (see also 7:19–21). Life is brutal and short, and any tiny sins committed during its course could not possibly be punished so grotesquely as Job has apparently been punished. Besides, God has made things like this, has made human life brief and hard, has fixed the short span of human life. The best thing God can do for Job now is clear out!

But Job is not content simply to command God to get off the stage. Job finds something more unsettling, more sinister about the ways in which God has created things (vv. 7–12). These terrible truths are more proof, if any were needed, that the universe of this God is a crazy place. Trees have far more chance of long life than humans. When humans' brief and brutal lives come to their inevitable ends much too soon, no amount of water can bring them back, no amount of tears or anger or work will enable them to return from the place of death. The unfairness of it all is breathtaking!

After this stinging sarcasm, Job has another burst of wild imagination. The picture he draws in verses 13–17 can only be said to be ludicrous on its face, given the traditional understanding of death and life that Job has earlier enumerated. He has challenged God to meet him in court to answer his charges (chap. 9). In that chapter, too, Job had a brief burst of imagination (9:33), where he envisioned the possibility of an umpire who would make a meeting with God feasible. Though he quickly gave up on the notion, it was an indication that Job will stop at nothing to gain his vindication at the hands of God. I see 14:13–17 as another imaginative scene where Job tries to describe a way that he can have his day in court with God.

Job describes a remarkable scenario. Because he knows that human life is short and harsh, and that death is the absolute end of that life,[7] his desperate mind moves to think the unthinkable. His fevered reasoning goes like this: Since God is currently furious at Job, has for some unknown reason become Job's implacable enemy, Job suggests that God place him in Sheol just long enough to allow God's anger to cool. Before God does this, however, it is crucial that God make Job's Sheol stay of a limited duration by appointing a time for Job's return. After all, under the normal circumstances of human life and death, Sheol is a place not subject to round-trip tickets! Job reminds God of that certain fact with the rhetorical question of verse 14a, the answer to which is no.

Then in verse 14b Job returns to his imaginative plan. Once God has placed Job in Sheol, and has gone off to lose the divine anger, Job would wait patiently in Sheol "until my change would come." The "change" Job wants, of course, is his release from Sheol, his return to life, a reality that can only come from the power of the creator God.

To effect Job's release, God would call, and Job would joyfully answer. The dialogue might go something like: "Job! Job! Where is my old friend, Job? Job, all is forgiven. Come back to the world of the living!" And Job would say, "Here I am, God, in Sheol where you put me. Has your anger cooled? You sound like your old self again. Let's try to make a fresh start together!" As they stroll, Job finally has his time with God, a time where he convinces God that God must act differently from now on; God's obsession with Job's every sin must stop! To ensure this new activity of God, Job urges God to take whatever sins Job may have committed and "seal them in a bag," or better yet, "cover them over." One can imagine God and Job, wreathed in smiles, gazing lovingly at one another, moving off the stage together, as the orchestra swells in the background and the credits engulf the scene.

Unfortunately for Job, just as happened to him in chapter 9, his imaginative enthusiasm for his plan soon wanes as the painful reality of his life crashes in on him again (vv. 18–20). The overpowering might and unrelenting antipathy of God drives Job's imaginative hopes right out of his mind. God is not going to hide Job in Sheol and then long for him with deep love and devotion! Just as certainly as mountains crumble and waters rework the shape of every landscape, so God always and inevitably destroys all human hopes.

Yes, there is pathos here, and weariness, but there is more. Job is bitter and sarcastic and furious in his helplessness before this divine monster who has tormented and destroyed him. But even in this helplessness, Job refuses to be reduced to a sniveling and pathetic victim. He continues his rage at God with the final and unconquerable hope that God *will* finally listen to him and *will* finally come to him.

Job's words are the last in this first cycle of speeches. Job sounds ready to be defeated, but he goes down fighting, proclaiming his innocence and accusing God of malfeasance and the misuse of divine power. And yet, this drama is far from over. The poet has no intention of leaving Job croaking his sarcastic fury into a silent universe. Nor have Eliphaz, Bildad, and Zophar run out of words in their attempts to defeat Job, to put him in his place, to prove him wrong and a blasphemer. And God has yet to speak, though it seems foreordained that God will do so. This drama cannot end in chapter 14, and it most certainly does not.

Comment

Where are we at the end of the first cycle of speeches? Let us revert to our analogy of drama, as we assess our understanding of the play at the end of what might be called Act 1. Job has staked out his position with vigor and force. He is essentially innocent. Not that he thinks he is sinless. But whatever sins he may have committed, either by things done or left undone, by words spoken or words not spoken, could not by any measure have brought on the calamities that he has had to endure. Because he believes that God indeed is the source of all things in the universe, and can be expected to reward the righteous and punish the wicked, the obvious conclusion to Job is that God has at best made a mistake in his case, perhaps confusing him with someone else (perhaps *Yam*; see 7:12), or at worst is a brutal and malicious beast who kills and maims indiscriminately and enjoys the mayhem to boot (9:22–24). As the act progresses, it appears that Job is inclined more and more to the latter view.

The friends are horrified at his words and try each in his own way to combat Job's heresies. The stately Eliphaz shares with Job a heavenly vision, designed to tell Job that his claims to innocence are, in the very nature of the case, impossible. Further, Eliphaz attempts to help Job reconcile with his suffering by reminding him that God only brings such suffering to those whom God particularly loves. The erudite Bildad, dusty books of traditional wisdom opened before him, tells Job of the past's great truths, truths that always give the lie to Job's absurd statements about God and himself. Zophar of the deep and mysterious knowledge urges Job to give up his claims to any sort of wisdom, all of which is reserved for God alone.

All along the course of these speeches, I have tried to indicate a few of the many examples of places in which words and phrases uttered by one speaker were used against that speaker, or even other speakers, in the attempt to hold other speakers up to ridicule. All four of our actors seem past masters at this skill, and the poet certainly knows the way around a supple use of the Hebrew language.

What does the stage look like as the curtain rings down on Act 1? I see the four characters in a line across the stage. The tall, bearded Eliphaz gazes at the distant horizon, perhaps hoping for another vision with which he can set this terrible Job straight. Yet he is also marshalling his faculties for another speech that will open Act 2. Because his first speech has been so ineffective, much to his shock and chagrin, Eliphaz is trying to think of different ways to approach Job in order to prove him wrong. Bildad, disheveled in his academic gown, his mortarboard askew, is especially amazed that the ancient texts that have been his life have had so little effect on Job. He is puzzled, as academics who are disagreed with often are, and he looks right at Job with a quizzical air, formulating his next speech that he hopes will prove devastatingly powerful and will end the debate in victory. Zophar, his beautiful suit still immaculate, gazes at Job with the beatific smile of one who is only momentarily cowed. He knows for certain that his truth will eventually win out, because it is God's truth, against which no human can ultimately stand. All three have been stung by Job's statement that they are liars, but each soon overcomes the shock; they know that it is Job who is the liar and soon, they hope, Job will also know it.

Job sits in the spotlight at center stage. The only sound is the scrape, scrape of the sharp-edged piece of pottery Job still uses to ease his suppurating sores. Some of those sores look as angry as Job sounds, as red-rimmed as his eyes, moving toward infection. Job's robe is little more than a filthy loincloth now, barely covering the private parts of his wasted body. His part of the stage is littered with dirt and old bones and trash. The three friends are far enough away to be clear of this filth. The look on Job's face is complex. He is defiant but in pain, not simply physical pain, although that is real enough. There is the equally insufferable pain of isolation and hatred. But the eyes are the key. The light is not out in Job's eyes. They take in the friends one by one as the curtain descends. He knows he is not through with these friends, but just before the audience's view is blocked by the curtain, Job's eyes look directly at the audience as if to say, "This is not all, my friends; the pain and the struggle are not over. Bear with us as we move deeper into the maelstrom of life and the mystery of God. Go, but not in peace. And then return, for there is much more to be heard."

CHAPTER 4

The Second Cycle (Job 15—21)

Job 15

Arguably, a different Eliphaz speaks this time. Dramatically, it could hardly be otherwise. The commanding visionary who spoke first with the assurance of certainty must have been severely shaken by the acrimonious dialogue that followed his address. Far from repenting, Job has rather grown louder in the conviction of his innocence and in his accusations that God is unjust and monstrous. Eliphaz has grown defensive under the Joban onslaught; he now realizes that Job will not readily agree with him or with his two friends; because that is so, something must be done, and quickly, to shut the little arrogant blasphemer up. True religion is at stake, not to mention the reputation of the respected Eliphaz.

The tone of his second speech clearly indicates his desperate urgency (vv. 2–3). In chapter 4 Eliphaz began his speech with what sounded like deference and gentlemanly concern, even though I argued that his words were only a thin smokescreen for overt cruelty. All traces of the niceties of polite society have disappeared here. If Eliphaz' goal in the first address was the conversion of Job in order to bring him back into the good graces of God, his goal now appears to be nothing less than the complete defeat of Job and his scandalous ideas.

In the long speech of Job just concluded, he has several times used the words "wisdom" and "wise." He has begun the impassioned speech by averring that the so-called "wisdom" of the friends is only worthy of his deepest scorn (12:2) and has gone on to say that their greatest "wisdom" would be to keep quiet (13:5). Eliphaz has been stung by these cruel jibes and has assumed that Job considers himself to be "a wise person." But this can hardly be so, says Eliphaz, given the ridiculous words that keep spewing from Job's mouth. Such words are little more than "wind," and their source is a bellyful of the "east wind." "Windy knowledge" is empty, insubtantial, invisible, finally "useless" and "worthless," ultimately dangerous. Job's empty rantings are a serious threat to the maintenance of true religion. Of course, Eliphaz can see Job's words for what they are, the ramblings of a badly deluded fool. But think of those who are not so strong in the faith as is the wondrous Eliphaz. Just as Paul would later warn his Corinthian friends to be careful not to "become a stumbling block to the weak" through their flagrant eating of the tainted sacrificial meat (1 Cor. 8:9), so Eliphaz demands that Job curb his wild words, which will certainly "diminish meditation before El." This is so, says Eliphaz, because it is not wisdom and knowledge that inform Job's words, but his profound wickedness. Eliphaz then proceeds to give a dazzling display of the dialogue's technique as he demonstrates just exactly how Job's own words have condemned him in the eyes of Eliphaz. I will offer only two examples.

The most blatant example of Eliphaz' technique is found in 15:6. "Your own mouth makes you wicked, not I," shouts Eliphaz, recalling Job's claim of 9:20, "if I am righteous, my own mouth would make me wicked." Job said that whether he was righteous or wicked finally made no difference, because God would somehow twist his words into condemnation. Eliphaz retorts that God has no need to twist Job's words at all, because those very words are themselves signs that Job is wicked.

Eliphaz becomes absurdly snide in the second example (vv. 7–9). With a reference to some myth of a "first man," Eliphaz snaps that Job is hardly the subject of the myth. (For a manifestation of this myth in the Hebrew Bible, one can read Ezek. 28:11–19, wherein the prophet skewers the king of Tyre for his pretensions, telling him that his doom is sealed.) In the second line of verse 7 Eliphaz borrows the words of Proverbs

8:25b, words used there to describe the birth of primordial Woman Wisdom "before the hills," in order to tell Job that he is hardly the equivalent of that great figure who was with God at the creation of the world (Prov. 8:22–31). Job is neither the First Man nor is he Woman Wisdom; he is just Job, foul and blasphemous sinner.

Eliphaz ends his second speech with a lurid description of the certain fate of the wicked (vv. 17–35). The most obvious difference between this second speech and his first of chapters 4–5 is that there is nowhere here any hope for the repentant sinner. Dramatically, especially with regard to the characterization of Eliphaz, this sharp change must be seen as the result of the impatience of Eliphaz in the face of the recalcitrance of Job. Eliphaz is furious, and his usual calm demeanor and his legendary self-assurance are fading fast. His words in this second speech are strident, not reasoned, and overtly cruel, rather than subtly so. In 12:7–8 Job had challenged his friends to "ask the animals who will teach you." Now in 15:17 Eliphaz confronts Job with his, Eliphaz', knowledge, not gleaned from animals but from "sages," great wise folk like Eliphaz who have special access to the world's truths. And all of this knowledge is designed to say one thing: All wicked folk are rightly and roundly condemned by the world and by God. And, as the reader has come to expect, Eliphaz couches his descriptions of the wicked's demise in words and phrases gleaned from the speeches of Job.

In 15:22 Eliphaz says of the wicked, "They do not believe that they will return from darkness." Any number of times Job has spoken of his certainty that he is going to the place of darkness, never to return (see especially 7:9–10; also 10:21–22; 14:11–12). In 7:11b Job had said that he would "speak in the anguish of my spirit." Eliphaz says of the wicked in 15:24 that "distress and anguish terrify them."

These examples should suffice to indicate that Eliphaz has designed his grim-fate-of-the-wicked speech around both the experiences and the words of Job. Eliphaz does in his speech what he says Job has done in his speeches. "Your own mouth makes you wicked, not I," he says in 15:6, and in verses 20–35 Eliphaz fulfills his claim by creating a clear picture of the fate of the wicked one, Job. Anyone listening attentively to Eliphaz' words must not fail to hear what the old visionary is about: He is fixing Job among the wicked, and he does so in a tour de force of Joban language and Joban circumstance.

Comment

There is really nothing new in this second speech of Eliphaz' in terms of what he has to say. Indeed, he nearly repeats himself verbatim at several places (see, e.g., vv. 14–16). His basic interests remain the same: He is wise and Job is not (vv. 9–10); God is offering consolation to those who will listen, some of which comes in the form of Eliphaz' own words (v. 11); human beings are all evil in God's sight, and hence so is Job (v. 14); God trusts no one, so God does not trust Job (vv. 15–16); the wicked will always receive just what they deserve, and Job is the world's best example of that fact (vv. 20–35).

What is different is the tone of the speech. It is rife with sarcasm and invective; its language is as intemperate as Job's rantings against God and friends. Eliphaz has been deeply pricked by Job's cruel words against him and his companions in chapters 12 and 13, and he is now intent on destruction rather than restoration. The evangelical Eliphaz, deeply concerned to bring the lost sinner back to the fold in chapter 5, is now bent on annihilation of the cancer that Job represents. But as in all fanatics, there is the undercurrent of desperation in Eliphaz. It is no longer merely one sinner he faces; Job is nothing less than the earthly manifestation of some evil principality and power who, if left to do his worst, would threaten everything that Eliphaz holds dear. Job must be more than defeated; he must be destroyed.

So, how does Eliphaz look now? His calm is gone; his visionary countenance is clouded with rage; his vaunted control has been shattered by one he cannot seem either to fully understand or to defeat. For perhaps the first time in his distinguished life, Eliphaz is not the master of a situation. His sumptuous robes are wrinkled, his tall hat hangs a bit askew. He looks much older than when this dialogue began; his eyes are red-rimmed, deeper-set somehow, rheumy. He ended his first address with a grand rhetorical flourish and moved away from Job to the sound of great applause, at least in his own comfortable ears. But the end of this second speech is snide, overtly cruel, malicious, sadistic. The words come out in a snarl, not in the rounded and deep bass of the practiced orator. In short, Eliphaz is on the run of his theological life, and he shows the signs of a cornered beast, lashing out in all directions, hoping to score a random point or two in a wild flailing of words.

I think he looks at Job differently too. Oh, he is more convinced than ever that Job is a very dangerous creature, and he sets himself the task of getting rid of him as quickly and completely as possible. But I think a sort of grudging admiration shadows Eliphaz' face, also. Job is a new and remarkable creature, evil but unrepentant, seemingly unaffected by the ancient truths, unmoved by the old words. Just what sort of creature he finally may be is uncertain to Eliphaz, but Eliphaz eyes him with disdain and fear and wonder at the same time.

Job 16—17

Job responds with deep scorn and withering fury to the exhausting sameness of the ideas of Eliphaz. But with Eliphaz' own loss of patience and his veneer of politeness, Job has even more reason to react to his words with genuine and justifiable anger (vv. 2–3). As in 12:3, Job announces early in a speech that he has heard or knows "things like these." What he appears to mean each time he employs this generic reference is that the ideas expressed over and over by the friends are all well known and well worn. It is a commonplace among readers of the book of Job to state that the friends represent a kind of caricature of some of the ideas expressed in the book of Deuteronomy. There are certainly many passages in that book that readily lend themselves to a one-sided, mechanical reading. For one example, in Deutremony 5:33 we read, "You must follow exactly the path that the LORD your God has commanded you, so that you may live, and that it may go well with you, and that you may live long in the land that you are to possess." That statement seems clear enough when read out of its broader context. "If you do this, these things will follow automatically." It takes little thought to see how such a sentence could be quoted as a summary of a "bumper sticker" way of life that leads to inevitable rewards or punishments. However, when seen in the light of the remarkable verses of Deuteronomy 7:7–8, the simple "tit for tat" understanding of 5:33 needs to be reevaluated completely.[1] Still, Job must have such familiar proverbs in mind as he speaks scornfully of "things like these."

"Troubling comforters are you all!" shouts Job, and given what we know now about the cruel intent of the friends, we would surely agree with his assessment. As "comforters" these friends are rank failures. But, of course, if my reading of their intent is correct, they had no interest in bringing comfort to Job in the first place. And so Job retorts that these so-called friends are little more than "troubling comforters," or more literally said, "comforters of trouble," a kind of oxymoronic charge. If "trouble" is what they are out to produce, they are hardly comforters at all. They in fact spew trouble instead of comfort, because that is what they wanted to do the minute they saw Job sitting alone on his putrid ash heap.

Job follows up his salvo of 16:2b with a direct retort in verse 3. Eliphaz had begun his more prickly second speech with the accusation that Job's words were based only on a "windy knowledge" (15:2). Job here says that the friends' words are themselves nothing but "wind." "What agitates you?" he asks. Given his earlier use of this word in 6:25, his question here is not fully serious; he knows precisely why they are agitated. He has pricked them deeply, and their mounting fury is a direct result of Job's complete refusal to admit the value of their harangues.

Then Job sees himself as bereft of all visible means of support, whether friends or God. In a series of astounding metaphors, Job portrays his God as: (1) a divine plastic surgeon who has "shriveled him up"; Job appears aged beyond his years (v. 8); (2) a wild beast whose teeth have "gnashed" and "torn," whose eyes have "sharpened," that is, "peered with intent to destroy" (v. 9); (3) a bloodthirsty warrior who "breaks in two" and "dashes in pieces" the enemy (v. 12a,b); (4) a terrible archer who sets up the target, but who then "slashes the kidneys open" with a sword, pouring the kidney's liquid on the ground, and showing no mercy to the wounded one by "attacking again and again" (vv. 12c–14). Job has used several of these metaphors before, but not in the highly pictorial and concentrated way we find them here. One can imagine the horror with which the friends listen to these words, recoiling from their fury as if struck physically in the face!

Job makes these wild accusations of his God despite the fact that he believes "there is non-violence on my palms" and "my prayer is pure" (v. 17). He does not simply avoid acts of violence; he is an active doer of nonviolence, as his detailed comments in 29:11–17 make plain. The basic meaning of "violence" in the Hebrew Bible is the "arbitrary and autocratic appropriation of what belongs to God or one's neighbor."[2] This definition is made more specific in a passage like Jeremiah 22:3, where the word means the brutal exploitation of the oppressed of a community, the aliens, widows, and orphans. Job states clearly that he is most certainly not to be classed with those evil ones who do violence. He is a person who has gone out of his way to help those very people who are exploited by the doers of violence. And because Job is a doer of nonviolence, he certainly ought not to have received the attacks of God.

Not only is Job a purveyor of nonviolence, also his "prayer is pure." This statement is in direct contradiction to the claims both of Bildad (8:6) and of Zophar (11:4). Eliphaz, too, denied that any human being can be "pure" in 15:14. Job has not done anything to deserve the attacks of God; even more, his exemplary behavior should have led to reward. The reader should remember that Job is not here claiming that he has never done wrong. By saying that his prayer has been "pure," he does not announce some kind of sinless perfection. The actions of this warrior-like, bestial God are plainly incommensurate with any actions Job may have committed.

And so again Job finds himself at a complete impasse. He rejects outright the friends' disgusting and unproven charges that he is a foul sinner. Yet he can hardly deny that the God who is master of the universe is using his shrunken body for surgical experiments and a grisly target of swords and arrows. Earlier in chapter 9, Job found himself in a similar position, having said that God was attacking him and having announced that God was finally a sadist, destroying both righteous and wicked and laughing as all died under the divine assault. He then, however briefly, imagined an umpire, a mediator, who might make possible a discussion between Job and God that would lead to some answers. But as quickly as the umpire was imagined, he disappeared from Job's radar screen. But once again, Job's imagination is quickened as he dreams of another figure who could be his advocate against a God who has become his adversary (vv. 18–21).

This passage is filled with both tantalizing suggestions and thorny difficulties.[3] I am sorry to say that verse 20 is nearly unreadable in the Hebrew text; any translation is at best a guess. Because that is so, I will leave the verse out of my discussion. Still, the gist of Job's imaginative flight can be gleaned.

Job first reminds the reader of an infamous story from the lore of the ancients. The memory of Cain's murder of his brother, Abel, was an indelible one. After the murder, God confronts Cain with the deed, and his lie in the face of God has become a cliché in many languages. "Where is your brother?" asks God. "I do not know; am I my brother's keeper?" Cain's sneering response carries the implication that he views his brother as little more than an animal. God's response to this appalling deception is anguish. "What have you done? The voice of your brother's blood is crying to me from the ground" (Gen. 4:9–10). Job draws a strong identity between his own innocence and that of his ancestor Abel. By connecting himself to this ancient and memorable crime, Job announces again that something truly terrible is happening in the universe. No longer is God the one who hears the outcry of the oppressed and comes to save; God has astonishingly become the oppressor, and Job is thus forced to look elsewhere for help against the divine enemy.

And then, as he did in chapter 9, Job turns from the friends and from God toward…whom or what? Many commentators assume that Job's advocate is God, but such a claim makes a mockery of the words of the text. Job says quite clearly that this heavenly witness "will argue with Eloah" just as human beings do on behalf of their friends. In that light, Job cannot be talking about God as his witness, unless one assumes that God is arguing against God! Amazingly, some commentators say precisely that. In this context, it is hardly possible that Job imagines God to be his witness.

Job has here upped the ante over his desire for an "umpire" in chapter 9. He now no longer desires only an impartial mediator. He now wants a "witness," one who is an "advocate." A famous example of the former word is found in Genesis 31, where Laban and Jacob end their long history of deceptions to one another with the "stone of witness," which is designed to "watch over each of them while they are separated" (see vv. 44, 48, 50, 52). Job wants such an authority in his struggle with God, someone or something to watch over the fight between them, who will come to help when either of the parties upsets the fair balance of the dispute.

The role of the witness is extended in verse 21; he will argue with Eloah in exactly the way that a man argues for his friend. The witness is a sort of attorney who listens to the charges of a client and then comes to the party charged with the offense and lays out the case. But here is more than an umpire, because this attorney is "in the sky," dwelling "in the heights." Thus, the witness lives somewhere close to God! The reader is reminded of the scornful words of Eliphaz in 5:1 where he challenged Job: "To which of the holy ones will you turn?" Is it possible that Job has now turned to one of the "holy ones"? As I have argued before, the friends have ironically driven Job to some of his wilder ideas and have again and again provided the energy that drives him to continue the debate.

In response to God's use of witnesses against him (see 10:17), and the belief of the friends that his scarred body witnesses to his evil, Job proclaims that he has his own witness, a powerful one who lives near God, who will settle this matter once and for all. And Job knows it must be settled soon, because his death is not far off (16:22). But Job's stance in the face of his certain death is very different than it was earlier in the drama. When Job first spoke of his death, there was a whining tone in his voice, a pathetic sound of the doomed victim (see 7:1–10, 13–16; 10:18–22). But in chapter 16, Job refuses to go quietly any more. He is certain to die at the hands of God, but he now demands that the injustice of the case not die with him. Hence the need for a heavenly (divine?) witness who will outlive Job and keep the case of his unjust murder alive in order that the injustice will not finally win.

Job is really quite magnificent at this important juncture of the play. He roars and rages like some ancient Lear on an ash-strewn heath and cries out for the justice of the universe, a justice that has been denied him so cruelly. At this point in the drama nearly every reader must have enormous sympathy for Job, very little respect for his so-called friends, and a gnawing distrust of the ever-silent God. We will have further occasion to address the identity of the reader with Job and what effects that identity will have on the ways the story may be heard and understood.

The heroic Job of chapter 16 sounds rather less heroic in the next chapter. However, the glimmer of his demand for justice, even after his own death, continues. Unfortunately, this chapter bristles with textual difficulties that have defeated many a concerted effort to tame them. Hence, I will confine my remarks to one place about which we can be fairly certain of understanding, a place important for our understanding of the drama (v. 10).

Verse 10 apparently provides some stage directions for the play. The three friends turn abruptly to leave, no doubt disgusted with the anti-God ramblings of chapter 16 and now the abusive crudities directed against them and their deepest convictions in verses 6–9. Job shouts at their departing backs and demands that they come back; he is not through with them yet, even though he will hardly find a "wise one" among them. The issue has quite certainly been who is wise or who has wisdom. If the friends have wearied of the struggle and have decided to leave, they change their minds, for the dialogue is far from over.

Comment

Job's fifth speech demonstrates his mounting rage coupled with a mounting unwillingness to die without a fight. God is characterized in especially brutal pictures, while the friends are accused of empty words of self-important and self-satisfied foolishness, untouched by the obvious pain and possible truth of Job's retorts. Job finally says with clarity that they are neither upright nor innocent, neither righteous nor clean-handed, for if they were they would have leapt to his defense against a universe gone mad. But instead they have stuck to their old foolishness and have attacked Job with unremitting fury.

The friends apparently thought they would leave the stage (17:10), but Job has called them back, demanding that they open their ears in order to hear at last the terrible truth of his life. But in the long run, it becomes increasingly certain to Job that these friends are not going to be of any help to him at all. Because that is true, and because God has inexplicably become his enemy, Job turns to another imagined figure, the heavenly witness, who will plead his case before the master of the universe, even though that divine one is at the same time the enemy of Job, who has made the need for the witness necessary. Yet what else can Job do? God is all-powerful, he thinks. Job is innocent, he thinks. God is the author of his life's tragedies, he thinks. Justice has not been served, he thinks. The author of the injustice must be confronted if the justice of the universe is to be maintained. But little Job cannot confront the mighty God, so he imagines a heavenly figure who can. And instead of turning his back on the possibility of such a figure as he did in chapter 9, here the possibility hangs in the air—quite literally in the air!

Job now refuses to die without calling out for justice, even after his own death if need be. As chapter 17 ends, the audience witnesses Job at the brink of certain death, his fist upraised, an initial cry of defiance stifled by the certainty of Sheol, a glance of scorn at the cowardly friends. The friends, possibly halfway off the stage, ready to leave this repulsive and abusive man to his own twisted thinking, have turned back toward him. The looks on their faces have hardened further into masks of horror and anger. There is only one reason for further speech from their lips; they aim to destroy Job. Bildad sets the tone immediately in his second speech.

Job 18

There is a basic problem in the understanding of the lines of verses 2–4. In verses 2–3 the pronouns are all plural. Thus, it does not appear that Bildad is talking to Job in those verses. We could say that verse 2 is directed to his two friends and is an indictment of their ineffectual speeches, all of which have failed to silence or to convert Job. But that leaves verse 3, which would make far better sense if Job were the subject of "you." I propose to read it thus, and I have changed the plural to the singular pronoun in verse 3b. Job is certainly the subject of verse 4. With that one change, the sense becomes clear.

Bildad is monumentally tired of this endless and fruitless debate, and he is more than ready to see it conclude. His hatred of Job spills over against his friends, whom he upbraids for their own wordy speeches. Verse 2b is a call for a reconsideration, a sort of time out. "Consider" he says; think again about what you are saying; *then* we can resume the discussion. Bildad may also be reflecting the near end of the debate that Job feared in the preceding chapter (17:10). The anger and frustration of the friends may have led them to leave, as Job's cry to them suggests. Perhaps Bildad's words are a call to reenergize the discussion, but after a suitable period of quiet where the three could gather their thoughts and begin the debate anew.

In verse 4b,c, Bildad questions Job's fantastic arrogance as he assumes that the entire world should be abandoned or forsaken by everyone due to the supposed injustice suffered by Job. This is reminiscent of Job's very first speech when he demanded that the dark magicians call up the fearsome Leviathan to destroy the world because Job's life was so terrible (3:7–10). What Job is proclaiming is nothing less than the end of the universe as a stable place in which to live. As far as Bildad is concerned, not "a single rock" will be removed from its appointed place as a result of Job's absurd demands. In short, Job will have no effect whatever on the world's certainty and God's maintenance of that certainty. As in his first speech, Bildad flatly rejects Job's basic notions about God and world and proceeds in the final seventeen verses of this speech to fix the horns of evil on the head of Job.

As usual, the Joban poet laces this "fate of the wicked" speech with verbal irony that connects the "general" fate of all wicked folk to the specific life and words of Job. One example will make the point. Toward the end of the speech Bildad turns overtly cruel as he says that the wicked one "has no offspring or descendant" and "no survivor where they used to live" (v. 19). The now-childless Job could hardly miss the point.

Bildad begins his speech with a call to his two friends to be more careful as they speak to Job, to reflect more deeply before they attempt to continue the debate. However, there is little indication that Bildad has reflected more deeply before uttering this address. It is quintessential Bildad, blunt, unyielding, and cruel, thinly disguised as a "fate of the wicked" general discussion but in fact an indictment of Job.

Comment

Little that is new is seen in Bildad's second speech. He begins by remonstrating with his two companions, urging them that they take more care in their reactions to Job. But he does not take more care. Job is the problem, not God. Job is the stupid one, not they. God is the just one, not Job. The world will be as it always has been, a place governed in strict retributive justice by a stable and predictable God. Job's absurdities will have no effect on that world or its God at all. His doom is sure; his fate is sealed. He will go to Sheol, writhing as he goes into the darkness that is reserved for all the world's wicked.

There is no room in the sanctified brain of Bildad for any new thoughts or possible questions. Job in 17:9 described him beautifully: In the light of Job's agony "the righteous stick to their ways." That haunting phrase should give some of us modern preachers pause. In the light of the world's agonies how many of us "stick to our ways," ways that we judge to be "righteous"? Is there any room in our sermons for the world's Jobs? Or like Bildad do we say one to the other, "Let's consider some more, and then we will speak"? When Job is in the congregation, we may need to do more than "stick to our righteous ways."

Job 19

Perhaps when Job called for his departing friends to "come back now" (17:10), he held out some faint hope that they might change their monotonous tune. Bildad's cruel speech dashed those hopes very quickly. And in response, Job returns to the offensive, and with pointed words gives back as good as he got (vv. 2–4). Though Job's words are directed at all of the friends (the second-person pronouns are all plural), he borrows the favorite opening gambit of Bildad (see 8:2 and 18:2). Job's reaction is laced with exasperation. Bildad had grown very tired of Job's "windy words" for which he "hunted" in order to say the most outlandish things he could imagine against God and the friends. Now Job returns the favor. It is the friends who are in the word business, employing words that "torment," "crush," "humiliate," all with the intent to attack and destroy without a hint of shame. Job names the debate for what it has been: a war of words, growing ever more lethal, proceeding without quarter.

At verse 4 he repeats what he has said many times before. He may in fact have done some wrong things. He admitted as much as early as 6:24, using the same word for "wrong" here as there. But we must not forget that Job emphatically claimed his innocence in 9:21; 10:7; and 16:17. But the issue is not whether Job has ever done something wrong. It is the disproportion of the response to whatever tiny errors he may have made.

After Job's rejection of the friends' tormenting words, he proceeds to turn once again to a brutal attack on God. The pattern of the speech resembles the one he uttered in chapter 16. There, as here, an attack on the friends' words (16:2–5 and 19:2–4) is followed by a brief lament about the disaster his life has become (16:6 and 19:5–7). That lament is followed in turn by a furious assault on God (16:7–17 and 19:8–12), and the speech ends with an imaginative probe for some figure who would keep the knowledge of the injustice done to Job alive even after his death (16:18–21 and 19:23–27). In the analysis of chapter 16, I presented reasons why the figure for whom Job longs cannot be God. The identical pattern of this speech of chapter 19 leads us to the same conclusion: Whoever the "redeemer" is that Job has in mind, that figure certainly cannot be God.

But before addressing that enigmatic passage, a few words about verses 13–22 are useful. The subject of these verses, although part of the attack on God, is decidedly different from the monstrous God images Job conjured in chapter 16. Job here accuses God quite directly of ruining his social and family life. He speaks of "family," "relatives," "acquaintances," "servants," "children," and "close friends." It is an abrupt change from the raw descriptions of God's violence in verses 8–12. Yet all of these monstrous disruptions in everyday life are no less acts of violence perpetrated by a God who seems to major in violence. Job's "bad breath" in verse 17 is merely on a continuum, resulting from God's more overt violent acts, but it is no less a result of God's violence.

In fact, it could be said that Job's angry cry of verse 7 summarizes the list of God's depredations in the verses that follow. As we noted earlier, "violence" in the Hebrew Bible is often the trigger for the angry and then saving response of God to oppression (see Gen. 6:11, 13; Jer. 2; Jon. 3:8). When Job cries "violence," he expects God to come and right the wrongs that have forced that cry from Job's lips. But Job's problem is the same as it has always been: The one who normally would come to right the wrong is the one who has caused the wrong in the first place! Such a catastrophic state of affairs now leads Job to his most astonishing, imaginative attempt to find a way out of his unsolvable dilemma. He will now announce the existence of his "redeemer." And with that announcement, we come to the most famous, and the most contested, lines in the story.

Job 19:23–27[4]

As is often so in this elusive book, when one most wants to have textual clarity, one seems to receive the least. That is certainly true with these infamous lines. Let me first offer a very tentative translation, as all translations of these lines must necessarily be.

[23] If only my words were written down!
If only written in a book, even inscribed
[24] with iron chisel and lead,
hewn out of a rock forever!
[25] Because I know that my *go'el* is alive,
and as the last one he will stand upon the dust!

^{26}And after this skin of mine has been flayed off,
yet without my flesh I will envision Eloah,
^{27}whom I, even I, will envision–not some stranger!
My inner life is consumed with desire!

In actuality, verses 23–25a present few problems of translation, while the latter five lines are filled with textual trouble. For my reading the key line is verse 25a, and the key word is *go'el*. What Job means by his living *go'el*, who is ready to rise up on earth with the apparent intention of acting in Job's behalf, needs some discussion.

The context of the appearance of this figure seems clear enough. Job wishes that his words, presumably his cries of injustice against God, would become permanent. First, he hopes for their simple writing in a book (v. 23) which the verb "written" implies. But the final verb of verse 23b changes the metaphor to one of incision, something cut in. Simple writing in a book is not permanent enough for Job's case; it needs to be cut into a more substantial medium than papyrus or vellum could provide.

But even that is not quite sufficient for Job's imagination! He finally hopes in verse 24 that his words of accusation will be "hewn out" of a rock for all time. It is common in connection with Job's intent here to refer to the famous inscription of Darius I, chiseled into a rock high above the road at the Iranian location of Behistun.[5] It is true that this 2,500-year-old inscription is still readable (at least the king's own name is still legible!) from a considerable distance. Here is in fact the most permanent way to preserve words known to the poet, and it will serve the poetic need wonderfully well. Job must have his words preserved for two reasons.

First, his death is imminent. Since he will not be around much longer to speak in his own defense, he needs an indelible record of his case. And he needs that record, second, because he has an advocate, a mighty *go'el* who will rise up after his death to confront God.

There are three possible meanings of the word *go'el*.[6]

1. Most especially in the book of Ruth, the word means a "redeemer of property." Boaz, a near relative of Naomi,

has the duty, as outlined in Deuteronomy 25:5–10, to marry Ruth, the Moabite widow, in order to ensure the continuation of the male line in Israel of the deceased Elimelech. The *go'el*'s role, understood in this fashion, would be not unlike that of the witness of Job 16:19. The redeemer would legally restore the broken community to its former equanimity, presumably by arguing Job's case before God and winning. Exactly what such a victory would look like is not even hinted at. In this light, the *go'el* would be in fact Job's witness, arisen to argue the case for Job.

2. *Go'el* is often used in the Hebrew Bible as a designation of God. Indeed, it is the Isaianic school's favorite name for the deity. No fewer than thirteen times (out of forty-four uses of the noun in the entire Hebrew Bible) is God called *go'el* in Isaiah, and ten of those are found in the poet of the exile, the so-called Second Isaiah (see 41:14; 43:14; 44:6, 24; 47:4; 48:17; 49:7, 26; 54:5, 8). Little wonder that many English translations of the Bible capitalize the word at Job 19:25, assuming that Job has no one but God in mind, that God so often known in the tradition as *go'el* (see RSV, NRSV, KJV, JB, "Avenger," CEV, "Savior"). I have already argued above that Job can hardly have God in mind as one who is about to come and be on his side. One can only assume that theological expectations rather than literary interests have led these translators to make their choices. In my reading, there is simply no way that the *go'el* can be God.

3. The third meaning of the term finds its locus in texts of Numbers and Deuteronomy. In Numbers 35 an extensive discussion is given concerning the existence of an office in Israel known as *go'el,* the "Avenger of Blood." This Avenger of Blood (*go'el*) is the community's executioner who is charged with the responsibility of strict and swift justice for a community riven by violent murder. Murderers who strike with intent to kill, whether with iron or stone or wood, shall face immediate execution by the Avenger of Blood (Num. 35:12, 16–21). This *go'el* roams the community, ever ready to exact

vengeance on those who with clear intent "push someone out of hatred, or hurl something at another, lying in
wait, and death ensues" (Num. 35:20). Once the murderer has been appropriately dispatched by the *go'el,* the
harmony of the community is restored. This entire idea
is based on Numbers 35:33. "You shall not pollute the
land in which you live; for blood pollutes the land, and
no expiation can be made for the land, for the blood
that is shed in it, except by the blood of the one who
shed it."

Is it possible that the "Avenger of Blood" is what Job has in
mind? Note several interesting points that make this a possibility. First, Job has already demanded in chapter 16 that his "innocent blood should find no resting place." If innocent blood
is not dealt with, the harmony of the community is impossible
(see, for example, Ezek. 24:7–8 where the guilt of Jerusalem
remains unexpiated as long as the blood of that guilt lies ex-
posed on a rock). Second, it is specifically the murderer who
"lies in wait" and who kills "with intent" who is confronted by
the *go'el* to pay for the crime. Job in 10:13 accused God of "hiding" the terrors unleashed on Job "in God's heart." "I know
that this was your purpose," Job says of God. And in 9:22–24,
Job accused God of killing both righteous and wicked and of
laughing while they died. This God, as described by Job, should
have to face the "Avenger of Blood."

If this extraordinary possibility be a viable one, let us sketch
the scene as Job envisions it. The impartial umpire of chapter 9
is now long forgotten as the imagination of the trapped Job
shifts into high gear. Even his heavenly witness is seen to be
ineffectual against God, the murderer and sadist. Here in chapter 19, Job first assures that his words of accusation will not be
lost in the dissolution of parchment nor the inevitable fading
of engraved plates. No, his case will be incised high on a rock,
outlined in illuminating lead for all to see; such an inscription
will last forever.

And now there arises a *go'el,* an Avenger of Blood, a colossus, an ancient Terminator, who comes from the frayed community to seek out the great murderer, the one who has killed
the innocent Job. The Avenger sees the case inscribed in the

rock and knows that his course is clear. And then, in a scene like some old-time gunfight at the O.K. Corral, the Avenger confronts God, the murderer, and destroys the deity with a great show of power! And best of all, Job himself will see it happen! Even after his "skin has been flayed off" and "without his flesh" (one possible way of reading the difficult v. 26), he will see God get what God so richly deserves. Job apparently anticipates some sort of post-mortem scene, but the text is so ambiguous that final certainty is forever beyond us. But, as verse 27 makes clear, it is no one else but Job himself who will witness the death of God (the NRSV's reading of "on my side" is unsatisfactory), and his deepest emotions are thrilled at the prospect.

Is such an outrageous reading even conceivable? Literarily, it is to me the far more likely reading. In what other way can Job hope to gain justice from a God who knows nothing of it? How else is a community, and Job within it, to regain their sense of balance unless this divine menace is dispatched? And the ancient office of the *go'el* is just the thing for the job. God has broken the community's rules and must pay the ultimate price. I am suggesting that with this ancient poet we find an early advocate of a "death of God" theology. But such a God as described by Job is clearly worthy of death, and perhaps needs to die in order that other, fresher ideas of God may find their place.

Comment

Job reaches a kind of summit in this chapter. It could be seen as a peak of absurdity, a promontory of despair, or a high place of extraordinary hope. He is trapped like a caged creature. His God hates and hunts him; his supposed friends detest him and wish him an early and painful death; he clings to the thin thread that God will finally see reason and admit that some terrible mistake has led Job to the disaster in which he is living. But chapter 19 shows just how close Job is to genuine madness. This God must be killed, because this God is monstrous, terrible in rage, and delinquent in behavior toward the world.

But in a very real sense Job is right! It is more than necessary that *this* God die! If God is anything like Job's portrayal, this God is finally no real God at all, but some kind of lower-case divinity who maims indiscriminately what has been made, who acts without purpose to destroy without reason. Job is quite right to want to kill off such a God, and all right-thinking religious folk should rush to join the murder. Surely, one of the things this poet is most concerned about is to get it right about God. And we cannot get it right about God until we remove those things that we have wrong about God. The God of the friends and Job at this point in the drama surely cannot be the God of heaven and earth, the God who in love chose the Israelites to be a special people (Deut. 7:7–8), who in love refuses ever to give up on them (Ex. 34:1–6). This mechanical God of the friends and this monster God of Job is simply not the God that so much of the Hebrew Bible knows and celebrates and honors. It must be that the poet wishes us to see just how far from that God this so-called God of the drama of Job truly is.

Any reader of the story must by now be ready for God to appear. Certainly nineteen chapters of "this sort of thing" should be enough. But, as God will ask Job much later, so the poet asks us now, "Gird up your loins like a warrior." The poet has more that we need to hear.

Job 20

From the beginning of this analysis, I have argued that Job and the friends have engaged in an increasingly acrimonious duel of words, characterized at times by subtle verbal play, while at other times employing quite bold and direct repetitions of words, the better to skewer the opponent. Zophar's second and final speech to Job uses both of these tactics (vv. 2–3).

"Indeed!" sniffs Zophar, perhaps the only word he can muster as he contemplates the fantastic speech he has just endured from the foul sinner Job. But he quickly recovers his tongue and says to Job that he will deign to answer him. He is right to say that he has "heard censure that humiliates" him. Job has tried to do just that more than a few times (12:2–3; 13:1–12; 16:2–5, among others). More specifically, Job has said at 19:3 that the friends have "humiliated" him "at least ten times." But Zophar is far from a loss for words in the face of Job's censure and humiliation; he still has his own deep "understanding" of God (11:7), the God who has an especially keen "understanding" of the wicked (11:11).

And Zophar's main target is still the wicked Job, whom he indicts in 20:9 with a phrase very similar to one found in 7:8, where Job laments, "The eye of one who looks for me will not see me." Zophar in typical fashion removes this sentence from its context and uses it to include Job in the ranks of the wicked. Certainly, "no eye will see you," Job, says Zophar, because "the cry of the wicked is short" (20:5), and, being wicked, you can rightly expect an immediate and grisly reward.

Verse 20:11 is an important one, because it appears to comment with ironic intent on two of Job's statements, those of 10:9 and more especially 19:25. Job's admission that God is in control of all life and death has a clear formulation at 10:9. "Ashes to ashes," Job intones, but he proceeds to charge that God's intent for the creation was always an evil one (10:13). Zophar takes this Joban claim and offers it as further proof that Job is wicked, one who will "lie in the dust" before his appropriate time, namely while "his bones are full of youth" (20:11).

But not only is 20:11 another attempt to class Job with the wicked by using his own words; it also seems to be a conscious parody of Job's burst of expectation for the *go'el* in 19:25. verse 19:25b reads: "and as the last one he will stand upon the dust." Verse 20:11b reads: "it (his youth) will lie down with him in the dust." The finality of the "last one" is contrasted pointedly with Zophar's obvious reference to Job's imminent death as a wicked one. Job expects the "rising" of his *go'el*; Zophar speaks of Job's "lying down." Job's use of "on the dust" pictures his *go'el* striding the earth as a colossus; Zophar's use of "on the dust" refers to Job's grave. In each particular, Zophar dashes Job's portrait of his champion *go'el*, whom he hopes will confront and kill God. For Zophar, however, there is only one figure in the heavens, and that figure is in the process of destroying the sinner, which is precisely what that divine figure always does without fail.

Comment

Zophar utters his last words with a nasty and gleeful snarl (v. 29). The "this" and the "such" are the terrifying portraits of the wicked that Zophar has showered on Job for the preceding twenty-four verses. After this deluge of description Zophar must have imagined that his arguments have at last won the day. Job is now seen for what he has always been: the foulest of sinners, masquerading as a righteous one, prattling on about the evil of God and the imminent death of God. Such aberrant foolishness needs to be stopped, and Zophar is convinced that he has done just that. He has no need to speak again, and he does not do so.

We might imagine the bluntly cruel Zophar, now convinced of his victory over the stubborn Job, grandly exiting the scene. He hates Job, as we know, but he has little regard for the breezily visionary Eliphaz, and probably has no time for Bildad either. He is a man supremely satisfied with his life and his thought and has no idea that anyone could think or live other than as his theology dictates. Precisely as in his first speech, Zophar has ended in an unanswerable dictum about the fate of the wicked. But after suffering the taunts and evil claims of Job's speeches of chapters 12–14, 16–17, and 19, Zophar has no doubt that blunt rejection is the only possible response he can make. And after that, he can do nothing but leave; he has no intention of dignifying this so-called discussion further with his lofty presence.

How does he look as he saunters from the stage? The beautifully coifed and dressed gentlemen we described above has been battered somewhat by this Job, although Zophar has done his best to remain above the fray. Nonetheless, as he departs, we can't help noticing that his fresh carnation has wilted a bit, that his tasteful tie has come slightly unknotted, that his matching handkerchief is not quite at the perfect angle in the pocket as it was at first. After all, Zophar has had it out more than a few times to mop his damp brow. Though his use of the handkerchief during his preaching missions is one of his more memorable and characteristic homiletical flourishes, he has found little pleasure in its use this time.

Most of all, Zophar is astounded that Job has not been cowed in any visible way. Zophar is used to winning, whether at bridge or at souls, and the fact that the sniveling, smelly little weasel is still there, and still talking, is a deep embarrassment to a person like Zophar. In fact, it looks like Job is getting ready to speak once again; Zophar has had enough. His dignity will not allow him to continue in this sordid affair. He turns to leave whence he came. With a practiced parting gesture of the right arm, he bids his inferiors good-bye, and with a final angry stare at Job he leaves to go back to people who respect the truth of the tradition, who respond with genuine warmth to a well-turned phrase and splendid rhetorical gifts. Good riddance, he mutters, as his Italian leather shoes disappear for what he imagines will be the last time. We will see him again at the end of our drama, but the role he will play there will be one he could not imagine in a million years.

What are we to make of Zophar? He, like his two friends, is a cruel and disgusting mountebank, puffed up with self-importance and an insufferable and arrogant certainty. He simply cannot listen to anyone but himself, since himself is all that he has room for. He speaks with ease and panache; he moves with grace, leaving people awed in his wake. We whisper in wonder when Zophar glides by, because he is exactly what many of us would like to be. A person of power. A person of awesome talents. A person who always rises to the top. A person on whose every word hang the hopes and joys of so many anxious and hungry souls.

Beware, says the poet. Would you really like to be like Zophar? A self-satisfied know-it-all, raised six feet above contradiction by a lofty pulpit or lectern or desk? The poet has tried in numerous ways to belittle Zophar, to cut him down to size, to uncover him for what he really is. Still, we covet his power, his clothes (Bill Blass dresses are no different from Armani suits when it comes to those who would be like Zophar), his prestige, his notoriety, his invitations. Do not think that Zophar disappeared finally so long ago; he is alive and often finds expression in some of us.

Job 21

As we reach the close of the second cycle of speeches, Job's address to the friends makes a shift. He is still sharp-tongued, and he still has no intention of admitting that they are in any way correct in what they say. But there is a different tone here.

There is a palpable shudder in these words to the friends, a pronounced horror. He wants these men to stop their cleverly mocking play of words long enough to recognize the terrible truth of things. The world is simply not, not in any way at all, like the world that they have assumed it to be. This Joban claim is not new, of course, but the way he states it is new. Job sounds weary of the cut and slash of witty repartee. He asks the friends to listen carefully for once to what he has to say, and after they have done so, if they are not convinced of Job's truth, they may return to their untrammeled mockery (vv. 2–5).

Job commands the friends to "listen very carefully." After you have done that, then you may return to your useless mockery. This is the word Job used to describe God's "mockery" of the dying innocent in 9:23 and the word used by Zophar to describe the foolish words of Job (11:3).

Another bit of stage direction appears at verse 5. "Face me!" he shouts. That is the quite literal translation of a verb based on the noun "face." Perhaps we should imagine that Zophar, who we said began his grand exit at the close of his speech of chapter 20, has nearly gotten out of earshot, so Job needs to raise his voice to call him back. And perhaps, as we witnessed in 17:10, the other two friends have either begun themselves to leave or have looked away from Job in horror or revulsion. In any case, he demands that they "face" him, look right at him, gaze at his wasting illness engraved in his aging face.

And when they look at Job, their action will be a ritualized "laying their hands on their mouths" (see Mic. 7:16 for this action as one of awe and astonishment). Job himself will perform this ritual as part of his response to the first speech of God (40:4). Job expects his friends at long last to see his problem for what it is: As he pled with them in 19:21–"the hand of the Almighty has touched me!"–he here again urges them to recognize that his horror is the work of God and no one or nothing else. Of course, the friends are more than ready to agree with Job in this; his destruction has indeed been the work of God, but a work called forth by the evil of Job. Surely, Job can expect no sudden change of the friends' hearts in response to this line of reasoning.

But perhaps these dramatic gestures were merely designed to capture the friends' flagging attentions, to get them away from their self-defensive attacks long enough to hear Job's plight and to feel his pain. The core of his argument in this, his seventh speech actually begins in verses 6–7. The true facts of human life are far different from the assertions of the friends. The truth is simple: "Why do the wicked live, grow old, and remain strong?" In 20:11, Zophar had declaimed that the bodies of the wicked, "once full of youth," will "lie down in the dust," obviously well before the allotted time of a human being, while their children must beg from the poor (v. 10). Job flatly denies that this is so. In Job's world the good are ravaged and die young, while the wicked, "filled with prosperity," go peacefully to Sheol (v. 13).

These wicked overtly flaunt their wickedness, demanding that God "leave us alone." They "do not desire to know God's ways" (v. 14). They brazenly say, "What profit do we get by praying to God?" Their obvious answer is, "None at all," so why bother! It must have been as difficult in Job's day as in our own to deny the basic truthfulness of these hard observations. Who could with a straight face deny that there are always times when obviously wicked folk live long, happy lives and die in silk sheets? And it may be even more true that perfectly lovely folk, loved and respected by everyone they meet, die young and in pain and are just as quickly forgotten, lying in unmarked ground.

And Job then turns his point around to confront the friends' ideas in another way. In verses 17–26 he questions the veracity of the notion that wicked folk actually see the retribution from God for their wickedness. "How often is the lamp of the wicked put out? How often does calamity come upon them? How often does God distribute destruction in anger?" (v. 17). Not often enough to make any sort of recognizable pattern discernible. The world's inhabitants survive in a place that can only be called absurdly random.

Job seals his devastating description of the world as he knows it in verses 27–34, closing the description with two powerful nouns that characterize all the speeches of the friends. The first noun, "emptiness," finds its classic use in Ecclesiastes, where the author sees all of life as no more than "emptiness," in fact "emptiness of emptiness," which apparently means something like "the most emptiness conceivable" (see Eccl. 1:2; 12:8, among other places in the book).[7] All of the many words of the friends have been no more than wind, completely insubstantial, completely without meaning or basis in truth.

The second noun is "treachery." This word can describe the violation of the sacred realm (Lev. 5:15), acts of faithlessness in the covenant of marriage (Num. 5:12, 27), or even violation of devotion to God (Deut. 32:51). Thus, for Job, the windy speeches of the friends are rather less than empty; they are violations of the truth, active denials of what Job can see and has experienced. In short, the friends are both empty and treacherous, and far from leading Job to comfort, they have added immeasurably to his unending pain.

Comment

I have suggested that there is a new tone in this speech of Job. It is blunt, and even at times snidely cruel as we have come to expect from him, but it is nearly devoid of the biting verbal ironies that have been so much a part of the dialogue to this point. It is as if Job has had enough of the bout and turns rather to direct counter-speech. "You have said this, but you are wrong. This is the way of the world, and that is all there is to it." There is a neatness here, a refreshing directness. Job has become the lecturer in the class "Human Life 101." Three pupils in his class are in real danger of failing the course, because against the unshakeable evidence of human eyes and ears, they have persisted in outright lies. Job gives a stern, yet generally unsarcastic, lecture to them in order to set them straight. After all, the final is coming up, and they need to be prepared by getting all the claptrap out of their heads.

He concludes the lecture with the harsh but honest portrayal of their knowledge as empty and treacherous, dangerously misleading, ludicrously false. His last line summarizes his appraisal of the sum total of their words: There is nothing left of all they have said save treachery. The final word to be said about their speeches is: emptiness, absolute emptiness.

One could imagine the dialogue ending here at the close of this second cycle. Surely, all has been said that could be said, both by Job and by the friends. We suggested above that Zophar may have already left; he says nothing more, in any case. Bildad will utter only six more lines, and their content is both disastrous and pathetic. Eliphaz gives it one more try. He still thinks he can win the day, but as we shall see, he gets hopelessly tangled in his own thinking and ends his speech in a kind of babbling nonsense. When Job speaks in 21:34, I sense a finality to the words, a weary summation of the whole of the debate. I think Job wishes the debate with the friends could now end. After all, as he says, his "complaint is not addressed to human beings." It is time, nay, past time, for a meeting with God. If Job's complaint is finally with God, the drama cannot end until God makes an appearance.

Much of the material that precedes God's coming is in several different ways problematic, and in a short treatise such as this one, I cannot begin to attempt to unravel much of it. Thus, the next portions of my commentary will be far more brief. I would suggest that this is so because little that is new will appear in the drama until the God speeches. I will point out various places that I find helpful to understand the whole of the play, its plot, and movement, but I will not dwell on niceties of interpretation where disruption and confusion have entered the transmission process, as both surely have.

CHAPTER 5

The Third Cycle (Job 22—27)

Job 22

This is Eliphaz' final speech, and he hopes to make the most of it. Job's address in the preceding chapter had a ring of finality to it, as if Job expects no more talking now, at least no more talking from the worthless friends. But Eliphaz feels he should try one last time to convince Job that he is wrong in all of his suppositions about God and about him. Given the tenor of his first two speeches, he can hardly allow Job to win the day with his monstrous claims about God. However, the speech begins in an odd and difficult way (vv. 2–5).

There is certainly passion in these lines, but understanding them fully is by no means easy. In Eliphaz' vision in chapter 4, the nocturnal visitor told him that "no one can be righteous before God" (4:17). This statement was based on Eliphaz' beliefs that God did not trust any of God's creatures, not even the angels, and that all human beings were "born for trouble" (5:7).

But now Eliphaz changes his central claim. Rather than arguing that no one may be righteous before God, he now says that no one can be "useful" to God. Eliphaz has used this word "useful" before. In 15:3, at the beginning of his angry renunciation of Job's "windy knowledge," he called Job's words little more than "useless talk," employing this word. He now says that not only does God not trust human beings, neither does God find any use for them. And just to make the point, Eliphaz repeats the word in the second line: "Mortals" are not useful to God and neither are so-called "wise ones." The portrait of God is of one who sits far from this world, untrusting and uncaring.

But Eliphaz goes further. God finds no "pleasure" whatever when one is righteous and gains nothing when one is upright. By these remarkable claims Eliphaz removes God even further from the world of humanity. God demonstrates no trust in humans, finds no use for them, derives no pleasure from their attempts at righteousness, and gains nothing from them when they strive toward uprightness.

If I understand Eliphaz aright here, if God does not in any way care about the actions of human beings, then has he not given the game to Job? Job had said in chapter 9 that God destroyed both righteous and wicked indiscriminately, and in chapter 21 had said that the wicked seemed far too often to live long and prosper. God never operated in such a rational way as to prove the contentions of the friends that God rewarded the behaviors of the righteous and punished the actions of the wicked. The world itself gave the lie to this absurd belief.

So Eliphaz says that God simply does not care about any of this. He has apparently been pushed to this amazing declaration by Job's bitter speech of chapter 21. Eliphaz tries to answer Job's constant drumbeat about God's malevolence toward him and the world by saying that God cares nothing about human behavior. But, of course, if Eliphaz is right about that, then all human behaviors are useless in God's eyes. That has been one of the terrible conclusions of so many of Job's speeches; it apparently makes no difference at all whether one is righteous or wicked, since success in the world has no relationship to being one or the other. Eliphaz has been driven by the furious Job to conclude something that has shown Job to be right after all!

But Eliphaz refuses to stop, apparently unaware that all of his words now mean nothing in the light of what he has just concluded about the uninterested God of the universe. Verses 4–5 lose all relevance. How could God be punishing Job for his supposed "vast wickedness" when God does not care at all whether human beings are wicked or righteous? Especially without point are his absurd accusations of verses 6–9 wherein Job is said to be the very epitome of a wicked oppressor, "sending widows away empty" and "crushing the arms of orphans."

The prophets of Israel believed that God was a God of justice and was most concerned with the powerless; God would not allow wickedness to go on forever.

But the God of Eliphaz does not act like that, as Eliphaz has just announced. Eliphaz' God does not care about human action. Thus, Eliphaz' indictments of Job are meaningless. In fact, it should now be seen that all of Eliphaz' words have been precisely what Job has said they were, so much "empty wind" (16:3). The awesome visionary has been shown up for the idiotic and confused mountebank that he is. And the remainder of this last speech is nothing more than repetitious nonsense. Even the final call of Eliphaz to Job to "be useful to God and be at peace" can only be seen ironically. Eliphaz said in 22:2 that "no mortal can be useful to God." Now to ask Job to "be useful to God" is the height of inconsistent and muddled stupidity. The pious claptrap with which Eliphaz concludes in verses 22–30 is only vacuous foolishness: "Pray to God who will hear you" (v. 27); "God saves the humble" (v. 29); "God will rescue even the guilty" (v. 30). All three of these religious phrases are meaningless in the light of Eliphaz' verse 2. He stumbles off the stage to the well-earned derisive hoots of the audience, who have had more than enough of this worthless man of vision.

Comment

"The supremely confident force of nature," thundering his certainties in the "sonorous tones" of "deepest bass" has disappeared. The rambling fool who leaves the stage after his final speech is a shell of his former self. His lavish blue robe is wrinkled, torn at the bottom. His tall, conical hat droops at a weary angle, the victim of the acrimonious debate. The visionary gaze has left the bearded face, replaced by the clouded and haunted eyes of one no longer so sure of mastery and success. The heel of one of the brocaded shoes was broken off sometime during the last pathetic address; it apparently snapped while Eliphaz was trying to punctuate his point with a loud stomp of his foot. Eliphaz is a beaten man, and the defeat is far the worse for one who had no thought of defeat when he first laid eyes on Job. As he departs the field of battle, he mutters quietly, complete sentences no longer possible, high-flown flights of rhetoric no longer available.

He began with clarity: "No human being can be righteous before God." Hence, any claim by Job to that effect is ruled out in the nature of things. But Job keeps saying it nevertheless, and no matter how often Eliphaz rejects Job's statements, no matter how awful a portrait of the terrors of the wicked Eliphaz paints, no matter how easily and completely Eliphaz connects Job to the class of the wicked, Job simply will not repent of the crimes that have brought him to this state, nor will he admit the truth of what Eliphaz has said. So, the speeches of Eliphaz move from supreme confidence and subtle innuendo (chaps. 4–5), to furious attack with direct accusations (chap. 15), to a confused ramble, thoroughly unaware of its own confusion (chap. 22). Eliphaz has been bested, and the audience has seen more than enough of his self-important blitherings and his cruel and snide assaults on the bereft sufferer. One can imagine a loud "good riddance" accompanying his leave-taking, perhaps punctuated with an assortment of rotten fruit.

Because I have suggested that Zophar has already left (see above), and now Eliphaz has joined him, only Bildad apparently remains on the stage with Job. Only Bildad hears the eighth speech of Job, a speech that reiterates and summarizes, announcing once again that Job has no intention of dealing with the three friends in detail any more. No, Job is ready to meet God, is ready to adjudicate his case with the divine defendant. Does Job imagine his witness is ready to plead? Does he expect the imminent appearance of a mighty Avenger of Blood to right the wrong done to him through violence? He does not say, but he does say very directly that the time for human debate has ended.

Job 23

Though this legal scenario is a reiteration of Job's increasing demand to meet God in a courtroom, it is the most concentrated snapshot of the scene we have yet received (vv. 2–7). The groaning plaintiff searches for the house of God in order to confront the divine one about the suit. Once the house is found, Job enters and finds the room of the court wherein he arranges the case, announcing to the court what it is he intends to prove, filling his eloquent mouth with superb arguments. God, who has listened attentively, then rises to answer the charges. The answers are reasonable and rational, completely understandable to Job. And God's answers are given without the excessive and wild force God usually uses in divine actions (see 9:4–10, 34). Job concludes the picture by saying that it is an "upright one" who will be arguing this case, and because that is so the only outcome of the trial can be the dismissal of the indictment against Job and the admission by God that God has made some sort of grievous error. It is of course Job who is the "upright one," as the prologue told us, but one wonders if he does not also include the witness of chapter 16 as a member of his legal team.

But the reader will note something very problematic about this legal scenario. Job's pleasant picture of a democratic and peaceful courtroom simply cannot exist for Job or anyone if the God of 9:22–24 actually rules the cosmos. Indeed, the remainder of chapter 23 suggests that no matter the beautiful picture of verses 4–7, Job is less than certain that such a thing could ever come about. Verses 8–9 signal the problem. Job simply can see no evidence of God's presence apart from the horrors that God inflicts on him and on the world. Unlike his now-absent friend Eliphaz, who claimed to have received a visitation from the heavenly realm in chapter 4, Job has again mocked that vision by saying that God cannot be so easily called upon (see his earlier mocking in 9:11).

Job ends his wild flight of hopeful imagination in verse 16: "El has made me faint! Shaddai has terrified me!" Chapter 9's call for an umpire came in the face of God's "dread" and "terror," but after the vision had faded, Job returned to his more sober belief that God had these terrors always "hidden in the divine heart" (10:13). Thus, there could hardly be an equal and legal confrontation with such a God, whose only interests are terror and the creation of dread. Job's hope for a heavenly witness in chapter 16 soon faded into his certainty of an imminent death (17:1) and his equal certainty that he was little more than a joke to an uncaring world (17:6f.). Even his belief in the existence of an avenging *go'el* in chapter 19 gave way to a grim appraisal of the triumphs of the wicked, capped by their elegant funerals and enduring memories in chapter 21.

And so it is in chapter 23. After the scene in the court, where the innocent Job argues with eloquence and persuasiveness with a calm and caring God, the reality of that God's elusiveness crashes in once again. How can Job argue his case with a God whom he cannot even find? At the end of chapter 23 Job is not much further toward a solution to his mess than he was at the very beginning of the dialogue.

Comment

In effect, Job has painted himself into a very small corner of the room of the universe. God, he says, is both his enemy and his judge, but is also an uncaring beast. All of his hopes are pinned on the fact that God is not like that at all, but what Job wants with one hand, he takes away with the other. He just cannot have it both ways, but it is precisely "both ways" that he keeps ever before us.

It is of some use to check ourselves now about our expectations. The play is plainly driving toward a visitation from God; it cannot end without one, but the author delays it a very long time. Part of the point of that delay is to allow the reader to build expectations about the visit. Those who strongly identify with the heroic Job will want God to agree with him and slap down the friends. Those who dislike the friends, but who are less than enamored of Job, will want God to put all of them in their place. And those who are troubled by the views of God expressed by all four speakers will want a God who is very different than any of them have imagined. Our eagerness for God's appearance will not lessen, but what we expect God to do in the context of the long debate may change as the delay of the visit continues.

Job 24

I treat this chapter separately from 23 even though it is put into Job's mouth as part of his eighth speech. There has been much discussion about whether this really could be a Joban speech in the light of Job's character, as it has been revealed to us up to now. This speech could be seen as a continuation and enhancing of Job's arguments in chapter 21. "Why do the wicked live on?" (21:7, NRSV) is the hallmark statement of that chapter, and Job extends that discussion here. It is a catalog of the deeds of various classes of evil folk (e.g., those oppressing the poor and the orphaned—vv. 9–12; lovers of darkness like murderers and adulterers—vv. 13–17). The problem, of course, is with verses 18–25, a classic "fate of the wicked" speech that sounds decidedly odd in Job's mouth. After all, his point has been that either righteous and wicked alike die indiscriminately (9:22–24) or that the wicked live remarkably long lives while the innocent poor and oppressed die much too soon, uncared for by God (for the former idea, see 21:7–16, and for the latter, see 24:12).

In my judgment, the disruption of the third cycle of speeches begins here. I have no intention of making still another fruitless attempt to unravel the tattered skeins that comprise this cycle; various attempts may be traced in any of the larger commentaries. The better part of valor seems to me to say little or nothing about speeches that seem so decidedly out of character for the supposed speaker. The Job we have been reading is not likely to have uttered 24:18–25; it is so unlike his speech that to believe it is an original one would do serious damage to the portrait we have been tracing. Of course, if he had undergone some sort of conversion to the views of the friends, or at least had begun to incorporate some of their ideas into his own, however little we have received a signal of that fact, we might then anticipate a continuation of this newfound traditional piety. The fact that we do not see any clear evidence of a new embrace of tradition makes me certain that these verses cannot be considered original words of Job. Hence, I treat them as misplaced and do not intend to examine them further.

Job 25

Here are Bildad's last words, all five verses of them. Again, various attempts have been made to incorporate either 24:18–25 or 26:1–14 into these five verses to make a speech of a more expected Bildadian length, but all such attempts are little more than trying to make a pig out of a string of sausage. I choose to read Bildad's speech as it is, because I can suggest good dramatic reasons why it may be so (vv. 2–6).

In this brief and bitter address Bildad makes his final attempt to silence Job once and for all. The recipe is one part fear and two parts abuse. In the process Bildad borrows words from Eliphaz, nearly verbatim, but employs them for his own particular ends. He begins by reminding Job, as if he needed such a reminder, that God has all the power, a power based in a "terrifying dominion" or a "dreadful rule." The "peace" God imposes in the "high places" is a kind of *pax romana*, a quiet based in power and force. After all, God's "troops" are unlimited. Bildad here uses a word from Job's speech of 19:12, where Job described God's "troops" as massing together against Job. You are quite right, Job, says Bildad; God's troops are coming and their number is uncountable. He then in verse 4 nearly quotes Eliphaz' famous visionary revelation in 4:17, but the line is decidedly harsher, more blatant, more hopelessly bitter in the mouth of Bildad.

The answer to both questions of verse 4 is a certain, Never; no one is righteous before God. This is true no matter what Job has proclaimed over and over again. Whereas Eliphaz has said that God does not trust even God's messengers and, of course then, did not trust any mortals, Bildad ups the cosmic ante by saying that even the moon and the stars, those early creations of the great God of Genesis (1:16), are not pure in God's eyes. And, like Eliphaz, he goes on to make a comparison between God's lack of trust of those cosmic creatures and God's lack of trust of human beings. The basic point is the same, but for him, mortals are nothing more than "maggots" and "worms."

The word "maggot" is a Joban favorite. In 17:14, in a sardonic little picture, Job imagines he might call the "maggot" his "mother," a grim way of announcing his death and the hopelessness that goes along with it. In 21:26 the "maggot" awaits both bad and good alike, as they both descend into death far too soon. And back in 7:5, Job says it is the "maggot" that has clothed his putrid and blasted body. Just so, shouts Bildad. That is all human beings are in any case, maggots! The word "worm" is found only here in Job.

What makes Bildad's use of these two repulsive and denigrating similes so striking is that they are the very last things out of his mouth in the drama! The bitterness and world-weariness of these final words are palpable. Eliphaz ended his speeches with a befuddled confusion of ideas. Bildad ends his speeches with a bitterly resigned announcement that, after all, human beings are only maggots and worms anyway, so why should we imagine that God either cares for us or trusts us for anything at all? How much do you care for and trust a maggot or a worm? All these grand words and clever speeches amount to nothing. I hardly hear a snarl in these terrible words; they are said with submissiveness. The speech is so short because after these words there is really nothing left to say. Macbeth is right: Life is "a tale told by an idiot, full of sound and fury, signifying nothing." With slumped shoulders, Bildad slowly exits.

Comment

The receding figure of Bildad is far different from the one we first encountered in chapter 8. The rumpled person of the scholar, so quick in argument, so certain in debate, has been reduced to this defeated man. His swift-moving, blue-green eyes are dulled, his academic gown with its proud doctoral chevrons sags noticeably, the mortarboard is nearly falling off the slumping head. The eagerness for debate and certain victory has been replaced by emptiness and hopelessness, the bitter truth of human meaninglessness in the face of divine dread. Bildad may have shouted his final words with a desperate defiance, but there is far more desperation than defiance in them. "What's the use," his sagging form seems to say, as it sidles off the stage. "So there!" says Bildad, but there is no "there." The world is empty, life has no ultimate meaning, and human beings are only invertebrate creatures without brains, without hopes, without purpose, without God. That we are all finally maggots and worms is the summation of the "condoling and comforting" of the three friends of Job. "Troubling comforters are you all," he said, and his judgment has proven all too correct in both senses of the phrase. Their attempts at comfort have been troubling, and at the last they themselves have become troubled and miserable. It is a most ignominious end for three persons who began the dialogue with the taste of certain victory in their mouths and who have ended silent and defeated.

Job is now alone on the stage. The spotlight is on him; the remainder of the playing space is dark. Perhaps there is a lengthy silence before Job speaks again. Is there anything more that can be said now? Surely, a speech from God is now called for. Job has vanquished the friends, but at what cost? If they are wrong about God, is Job right? Is the universe controlled (or not controlled) by a tyrant with a malevolent heart and a wide sadistic streak? Will no one come to announce to us the resolution of this awful state in which Job has put us all?

Job 26:1–4

These sarcastic lines are certainly a speech of Job, as he shouts at the friends who have retreated from the stage (vv. 2–4). One interesting characteristic of this rejection of the friends is that all the pronouns are singular. On perhaps two other occasions (see 16:3 and 12:7–8) Job used a singular address to attack the words of the friends, but most of the time he includes all of them in his assaults. It could be said that Bildad's quite disgusting and bitter speech of chapter 25 had especially pricked Job, who hurls his sarcastic taunts at the retreating Bildad specifically. Sarcasm does indeed seem to be a particularly appropriate response to the terrible final words of the second friend. They are certainly words devoid of "help, deliverance, counsel, and wisdom." And such idiotic and foolish nonsense could hardly have been spoken without some help from the outside; some unnamed "breath" must have formed these "wonderful" words in Bildad's mouth! Job is right! Bildad's final lines leave us all slightly sickened and definitely comfortless.

Still, despite the singular pronouns, Job's words here are perfectly applicable to the other two friends as well. These three verses well summarize his estimation of the impact of their words. In short, they have all been useless. (The remainder of chapter 26, vv. 5–14, is certainly not speeches of Job.)

Job 27:1–12

The first five lines of chapter 27 could easily follow the lines discussed above, 26:1–4. Here Job lays down his gauntlet and finally and utterly dismisses the friends and their supposed truths about him and about God (vv. 2–6).

Alone on the stage, illumined by a single spotlight, Job hurls his defiant words in three directions at once. He is shouting at the absent friends to make certain to them that they have not turned his thinking one iota in their direction (the pronouns of v. 5 are plural, suggesting the words are directed at them). Though the friends may be the primary object, we, the readers, are also addressed by Job. He wants us to be certain that his conscience is clear; nothing he has done in the past, nor any words he has uttered during the course of the debate, have brought him any regrets or remorse. He has spoken neither "wickedness" nor "deceit." Never, never will he abandon his "integrity." We know this latter word well by now. It was the first adjective used to describe Job in the very first verse of this story: Job is "upright," the narrator told us, and now Job uses the noun formed from the same verbal root, saying that his "integrity" is, and will always be, part of him. Given the evidence of the prologue and Job's own powerful avowal here, Job's integrity can hardly be in question, no matter how often the friends have tried to say that Job was little better than a lying blasphemer. And certainly Job is also addressing the silent partner in the dialogue, God, demanding that God break the silence and come to address Job's demands.

In the succeeding six verses Job calls down an imprecation on his enemy, whoever that might be, whether friend or God. Surely, he says, anybody with a brain in his head or eyes to see can testify to what God has done to Job. And what of God? "Does El hear their cries when distress comes to them?" (v. 9). Hardly! God does not care, does not listen, will not come. In these short strokes Job voids all of the traditional expectations of the God of Israel. The words are a kind of parody of the pivotal verses of the book of Exodus (2:23–25). Before God's deliverance of the slaves from Egypt, we are told that God "listens" to their "cries" and "comes down" to "deliver." That is all a lie, says Job. (Verses 27:13–23 are plainly not original words of Job; I thus do not comment.)

Comment

These verses really do have a sense of finality to them; surely *now* God will come! Job has hurled the glove down;

someone, and that someone must be God, given the defeat of the friends, must pick it up and agree to a time for the contest, a place for the hearing of the case. Unfortunately, ten long chapters separate what seems so needed now from the eventual consummation of that need. And again the reader needs to ask why there are these ten chapters still to be endured.

I repeat that the long delay both heightens the tension of the drama and allows the reader time to reflect even more deeply about how he or she would like the play to end, how he or she would like God to act and speak upon appearing. But still, what is to prevent a reader from merely losing interest in the story and moving on to another one? Is the delay too long? What is one person's heightened tension is another's overlong frustration. I admit to a certain amount of frustration at this juncture, because I feel that I am ready to hear from the Almighty. I am very glad that the cloddish friends have disappeared at last, and I have joined in on the chorus of boos that welcomed their departure. But I am nearly as weary of Job. He is insufferably self-righteous and insufferably arrogant, and perhaps at this point in the drama, insufferably pleased that he has driven the friends from the scene. My emotions toward him are complex: admiration coupled with disgust, awe mixed with deep displeasure, joy in his defeat of the friends along with a distrust of his motives and what he thinks he has accomplished. I frankly admit to a large measure of ambiguity toward Job right now; I am not sure just what I think of him or what I hope happens to him when God comes. But however much I want God to come, it does not happen yet.

CHAPTER 6

Job 28—37

Job 28

Though this chapter is ostensibly a continuation of the speech of Job in chapter 27, it is immediately obvious that this is a self-contained poem of the narrator and should not be attributed to any of the four speakers. It is a poem in praise of wisdom, employing the metaphor of the search for the rare and precious. It is among the finest pieces of poetry that the book of Job presents, but the real question is, of course: What is it doing here at this point in the drama? If 27:1–12 is seen as a final announcement that Job is innocent of all the friends' many charges and is not an appropriate target of God's merciless attacks, then a meditative reflection on the location of wisdom must be distinctly beside the point. Commentators have both waxed eloquent about its stellar beauties and cursed it for a crass intrusion. Such a variety of responses indicates that no final and irrefutable reason for its placement can be provided. Thus, my reasons can only arise out of the reading I am providing for the whole story; my understanding of the shape of that whole determines my understanding of the placement of chapter 28.

I assume that the poem is original with the poet of the book, and that two goals should be noted for its inclusion.[1] The key to both of the goals is found in verse 28. The long and exhausting dialogues have been attempts to find wisdom that will enable all to understand just what has happened to Job. This search has not been successful; at dialogue's end no one is any nearer to such wisdom than they were at dialogue's beginning. Words and phrases have been used as weapons, but wisdom leading to understanding has been nonexistent, despite many claims that wisdom was readily available to those who would act and speak aright (see Eliphaz in 15:8, Zophar in 11:6, Job in 12:2, 12–13, among others). The first goal of the poem, then, is a clear judgment on the preceding debate; that debate has been a failure, an interesting and occasionally enlightening failure, but a failure nonetheless. In reality, wisdom has not been found, because only one being knows where wisdom is: God. And because God gets the final word in the poem, God, through the words of the poet, reprimands Job and his three friends for their futile and tiring search for something to which they have no final access.

But that cannot be the only goal of the poet, for if it were, there would be little need for the play to continue. Chapter 28 could be seen merely as an orthodox no, both to the friends, who think they know more than they can, and to Job, who claims to know more than he can and who says the most ridiculous things about God based on that pathetically insufficient knowledge. The reason that there is another goal is twofold. First, the drama goes on, which must mean that the poet did not intend for this poem to be some sort of final word. Second, the poet signals that intention with an interesting choice of words in the key verse 28.

There is a second goal. In 28:28 we are led back to the very beginning of our story, verse 1:1. "Understanding," says the poet, is "to shun evil." It is precisely this phrase that characterized Job at the story's start: He "shunned evil." But that fact, along with his portrayal as one "perfectly upright," offered no protection for Job from an angry God, nor did it offer him any way to understand that anger and why it was directed at him. In short, for Job "shunning evil" is quite simply not "understanding." The orthodox answer of chapter 28, perhaps summarized by a shrug and a "God knows," is familiar and as comfortable as a pair of old slippers, but will finally no longer serve Job, who has in fact found no comfort from those who would hold to this party line.

Thus, the dialogue between Job and the friends may not have yielded the wisdom needed to discern the truth and is subject to a poetic reprimand for its final, unsatisfying emptiness. But there are other issues that are still hanging fire. The friends' arguments have been found futile and ridiculous, so the old orthodoxy will no longer do by itself; a smile and a "God knows" is not enough any more. This is so because Job has been described as one who has done all the things necessary to insure himself a good life, a life that ought to make him the model wise person, but he has received something quite different. Further, he has charged God with terrible actions. Neither you nor I nor the poet can ever again be satisfied fully by a calm "God knows." We want more, and the poet is intent on providing something more.

Job 29—31

The Job of this lengthy speech seems no longer intent on skewering the friends or in mounting another assault on God. He here participates in a traditional lament form from the psalms, crying out concerning the glories of the past (chap. 29) and the horrors of the present (chap. 30), and capping the act with an oath of clearance (chap. 31), which readies him for a confrontation with God (for other similar "protestations of innocence," see Ps. 7; 46; 17:3–5; 26:3–5). This speech is a summary of Job's position before his meeting with God, but the summation is necessarily different in tone, because the drama is in a different place than it was when the dialogue came to an end.

Job is now alone; the friends are gone and are no longer within earshot of his words. He need not direct his barbs at them any more. I have argued throughout this reading that it was, ironically, the friends who often gave Job the energy to continue a debate that he first wanted to end with his early death. But their angry and cruel rejections of his words urged him to new heights of rhetorical combat and led him away from a desire to die to a desire to confront God and to be vindicated, either by law or by violence. The words of this, his final, long speech, are necessarily devoid of his earlier combat with them, because that fight is over. But the desire to confront God burns as brightly as ever.

The summary of his location in the drama takes the form of a classic lament psalm with an added oath of clearance, designed to energize the appearance of God. The relationships between these chapters and certain laments from the psalter have long been recognized.[2] All the reader needs to know is that the entire effect of these chapters, both in their form and in their content, is designed to force God to appear, to come down and end the misery of the sufferer. Of course, the obvious and telling difference between Job and the sufferers of the psalms is that the latter expect God to come to deliver them from some external enemy, whether a foreign foe or a wasting sickness, while the former seems to expect God to come and vindicate him against God, whom Job believes to be his enemy. Nevertheless, the form of the lament is the perfect traditional vehicle to bring about a visitation from God.

The shape of the three chapters is quite simple. Chapter 29 describes the wonders of Job's past life: his vast honor among all people (vv. 7–10), his marvelous work on behalf of the poor, the orphan, the widow, the wretched (vv. 12–16), his active engagements against the forces of wickedness (vv. 17–20). In Job's glory days, he "sat as chief and dwelt like a king"(v. 25). Eliphaz accused Job of all manner of evil actions in chapter 22, but we see by these descriptions that Eliphaz' charges were false. Job has lived an exemplary moral life, a life outlined for us in the brief descriptions of the prologue, now here filled out and clarified.

But these days are gone, as chapter 30 describes. Job's honor has turned to scorn (vv. 1–10), the world's rabble have risen against him (vv. 12–15), his health has disappeared (vv. 16–17, 27, 30), and God has forgotten him and does not listen (vv. 20–23). But Job does not here name God as monster or beast. Verses 20–23 simply call God "cruel, silent, unmoving." These are the words of the psalms of lament, and they are uttered to get a hearing from God.

As Job enters this oath formula of chapter 31, he is in effect announcing that his innocence is absolute. If he has broken any of the moral demands of his community, he asks that terrible retribution descend upon him. These community demands include: a turning to "deceit" and "falsehood" (v. 5), sexual immorality (vv. 9–12), various kinds of unjust practices (vv. 13–23), greed (vv. 24–25), and idolatry (vv. 26–28), among others. Job avers that he has done none of these things, and by so stating he calls on God to come to adjudicate the obvious mistake that has been made by God's attack on Job's life.

There is a glaring problem with Job's use of this oath. An oath of clearance rests on the assumption that God is a God of justice and will not allow injustice to continue forever. Job, of course, again and again has denied this about God (see 9:22–24; 21:17–18; 10:7–13, among others). Thus, how could he possibly imagine that such an oath would have any effect, if the God of the universe is anything like Job has claimed?

My answer is that these liturgical chapters are another, indeed the last of, Job's imaginative flights, all of which have been designed to get the matter settled, one way or another. Job moves from umpire to witness to avenger in his attempts to find vindication. He now attempts a traditional liturgical act that in the past has brought about the vindication of God for traditional Israelite sufferers. No more here than in those earlier places is Job thinking with complete rationality. Would we expect cool rationality from a man stretched to the limits of human endurance, battered by his would-be friends, rejected and abused by the only God there may be? Job has one goal—to meet God. Any means to effect that meeting will be tried, including means that on their face seem quite absurd and impossible in light of earlier claims and ideas that Job has expressed.

That his goal is still that meeting is made certain by verses 35–37, which intrude in the midst of the formal oath. It is as if Job, while intoning the formal words of the oath, can restrain himself no longer and reverts to his more familiar tone of sharp demand. Here once again is the Job with whom we are familiar! Bold and decisive and demanding, he signs his charges against God. Then he requests a copy of God's charges against him, which he will then display on his own person. Afterward, he will answer the charges one by one, approaching the Almighty One as an equal. Thus, Job's final long speech is a mixture of liturgical formality and straightforward demand, but all created as the overwhelming means to bring about that for which Job has longed: the divine meeting.

As chapter 31 comes to a close, there can be little doubt in the mind of the reader that now, at long last, finally, God will put in an appearance. Job is ready, and we are more than ready.

Comment

This final burst of Joban imagination seems an especially powerful way to lead in to the long-awaited meeting between Job and God. The foolish friends are gone, and Job is prepared in every way he knows how to meet the Almighty. The fact that the meeting is once again postponed is a serious disappointment, and has led the great majority of commentators to condemn the author of the speeches of Elihu as an intrusive blowhard who has little if anything to add to the discussion. However one finally adjudicates Elihu's contributions, the frustration level rises noticeably when, instead of God, the audience sees a fourth friend enter the scene. If the speeches of Elihu are from the pen of the main poet, he does stretch our patience to the breaking point. I can imagine that more than a few readers have given up on the drama when they heard Elihu bluster into the story. If so, that was a great pity, for the poet still has important things for us to hear. But I fear we need to survive this Elihu, if we are to hear them.

Job 32—37[3]

These chapters, given over to the long speech of the fourth and quite unexpected friend of Job named Elihu, have been evaluated in several different ways. The majority of scholars relegate them to some sort of addition to the original drama, either as written by another poet or as a series of late reflections by the same poet. The poetry of these speeches is often said to be decidedly inferior to that which has appeared before, while the content of the speeches is usually described as repetitious, adding little or nothing to the discussion. In short, Elihu is regularly given a generally negative evaluation as a long-winded, pretentious interloper, who appears from nowhere and returns after his bloated address to the same unknown place. He is not mentioned in the prologue (2:11) or in the epilogue when God upbraids only three friends (42:7). Thus, while other scholars find Elihu's words very important for the story, most spend comparatively little time with him.

In the main, I find myself among the majority in my evaluation of this young friend. He is a hot-headed windbag; he is extraordinarily convinced of his own brilliance and the enormous stupidity of Job and his three colleagues; and he is certain that after he finishes, Job will be effectively silenced, God completely vindicated, and the three friends shown to be fools. The fact that none of these three outcomes occur may suggest that the general dramatic function of the appearance of Elihu may be as significant as, or more significant than, anything he may say.

For the purposes of my reading I will focus only on Elihu's first and last speeches, because specific attention to those words will uncover the reasons for his appearance. I believe that the poet we have been reading wrote these speeches with a particular dramatic intent in mind. Also, irony plays a significant role in the presentation as the dramatic intentions are played out.

Elihu's introduction to the story is in prose, reminding the reader of the beginning of the tale. Just as the information concerning Job and the disasters he suffers in the prologue is crucial for a proper evaluation of the poetic dialogue that ensues, so the narrator's prose introduction of Elihu is very important as we evaluate his poetic speeches that follow (32:1–5).

The central emotion of Elihu's introduction is anger. Three times we are told that he "became angry." The first use of this construction in verse 2 represents the deepest anger, because Job had "made his own righteousness greater than Elohim's." There can thus be no doubt that before Elihu utters his first words, the reader is convinced that he is angry, angry at Job and angry at the friends. We expect his words to appear in a flood, as if forced out of him like the venting of an erupting volcano. And so they do! But Elihu's own self-perception is strangely at odds with the character the narrator has just presented. He erupts all right, but the man we hear and see speaking is not quite the man he thinks he is; the narrator offers us the picture of still another self-possessed windbag (so especially Eliphaz) rather than the wise and patient dispenser of truth that the speaker thinks himself to be. The opening words of his address make this clear. Verses 6–10 and 18–20 are the heart of a laughable speech of self-introduction that for twenty-four verses tells the reader that Elihu is about to speak! No one could listen to Elihu for these twenty-four verses without laughing out loud at the monumental absurdity of it all.

After such a prodigious opening, it will certainly be difficult to take much of what Elihu says subsequently very seriously. More than a few commentators have discovered some sense of humor in the speeches of Elihu, but what is the point of humor just now in the drama?

I wish to use a very general Shakespearean analogy. The playwright regularly demonstrated the power of comedy in the teeth of tragedy. Lear's fool, Macbeth's drunken gatekeeper, Hamlet's Polonius are but three examples of humorous characters brought on the stage often at the tightest turns of the plot's tension. As Macbeth and his astonishing spouse drip blood on the stage, the too-loud knocking at the gate drives them off to their conscience-stricken room and ushers in the bilious porter, who releases tension at the awful moment and allows the audience to rest a moment before the next horrors appear (Act 1, Scene 2). In a different way, while the blighted Lear comes to terms with his mortality, the fool keeps the audience laughing and helps the troubled king reach a sense of tranquillity in the midst of the raging storms of his life (Act 3, Scene 2).

This, I believe, is the role of Elihu in the book of Job. He is a buffoon, but a buffoon unawares and is thus doubly ironic. We laugh at his inordinate pretensions, expressed through his unending words, but we may also laugh at the obvious fact that he takes himself so seriously. Elihu is the very last person in the theater to know that he is making nothing less than a fool of himself! For an audience growing increasingly impatient for something like a resolution, someone like Elihu may be the only character, save the deity, who could possibly appear just now.

But that is not quite all that should be said about Elihu. He does finally arrive at the content of his address, but after that immense introduction, the reader certainly expected more than Elihu seems capable of providing. In fact, there is nothing that we have not heard before from Eliphaz, Bildad, and Zophar. By the standards of the three friends' speeches, Elihu's words are very long, 136 verses after that twenty-four verse introduction. Elihu is, save Job, the speaker we hear most from in the drama; his speeches even outstrip those of God in sheer length. Yet, their prodigious length cannot hide a very simple and familiar content.

His theses are two: God disciplines people in order to turn them from possible further error (see Eliphaz, 5:17–26, for a crisper statement of the same idea), and God always governs with justice, without any exception possible (each of the three friends had made this point ad nauseum). These two theses well summarize the vast bulk of Elihu's argument against Job and comprise the essence of chapters 33:8–37:13. According to Elihu, Job should be learning from the disasters that have come upon him, and any claims on Job's part that God is unjust in any way are quite absurd and can be rejected out of hand.

And one more observation should be made. Elihu concludes his long expression of the absolute justice and hard teaching of God with a genuine rhetorical flourish that plays an important role in the plot of the drama (37:19–20). The overpowering mystery of God and God's refusal to come at Job's beck and call certainly will make it hard to have a court case. Can someone be sent to tell God that we want to have a chat? In these snarling sentences Elihu sneers at Job's desire to talk with God and at his certainty that God will eventually do so. Job needs to forget any foolishness that he will ever actually see God. After all, one cannot look at the sun when the clouds have parted (v. 21). Neither can a human being find God, nor receive a direct answer from God. That is precisely the reason that human beings are in awe of this God: Though vast with righteousness and justice, this God remains wrapped in mystery and cloaked in enigma. Even the very wisest of human beings will never catch a glimpse of God (v. 23); how much less Job, the foul and pretentious sinner! Thus, unlike the confusion, bitterness, and silence of the three friends, Elihu ends his 160-verse speech with energy, certainty, and an absolute conviction that he has spoken the very words that Job needed to hear. All that remains is for Job to admit that his claims for justice against God are wrong, that God always knows best how to deal with God's human creation, and that no meeting with this God is possible.

Unfortunately for Elihu, the next voice that is heard in the play is the very last voice Elihu ever imagined would be heard. It is the voice of God! The most astonished player in the drama is Elihu. As God launches into the first divine address, one can imagine Elihu slinking from the stage in genuine fright; all that he has predicted of God has been proven false. God actually answers Job out of a storm, saying nothing at all directly to those who have spent their time defending God with all their energy. Elihu leaves in fear but also with some anger, we might imagine. His long defense of God and rejection of Job, based on the mystery and unavailability of God, has turned to ashes in his mouth. This meeting is so contrary to all that Elihu has said, there is little wonder that he disappears from the drama completely. All that remains are the distant memory of his absurd introduction of himself and his final words about a God whom he obviously does not begin to understand. And so, at last, Job and God meet.

Comment

The role of Elihu in the story may be summarized as follows:

1. He is comic relief. His puffed-up introduction of himself to us is nothing short of hilarious, twenty-five verses of bombast and pretension that undercut anything of seriousness he might have to say.

2. Still, he does summarize two of the three friends' basic contentions about the ways of God: God wounds us to discipline us, and God is always just in divine action. Further, with his loud proclamation of the mysteriousness of God, God's unwillingness to appear at our call,

he emphasizes what so moved Zophar about God in his first speech (11:5–12).

3. His pompous address, loudly sounding the themes of divine inaccessibility and silence, ironically prepares us for the sudden appearance of that very God, completely accessible and not at all silent! The loud-mouthed know-it-all must have been shocked to his core to have heard the voice of God roaring out of that storm and must have beat the hastiest of retreats in its wake. No experience could have taught Elihu more clearly that his understanding of God was in need of serious revision. And in that, he becomes perhaps our spokesperson. Perhaps our vision of God needs a revision, too. Whatever we now expect God to say to Job, and we will address some possibilities in our next section, what God actually does say may hold some surprises for us no less than it does for Elihu and his three colleagues. Our glibness about God may need some fresh talk from God too.

We certainly cannot leave Elihu without dressing him for the play. As a young and ambitious firebrand, Elihu is "dressed down" for success. That is, he is classically casual, khaki pants, a color-coordinated shirt, Birkenstock sandals, Rayban sunglasses. His tan is golden, his hair a deep bronze, carefully tousled, through which his strong hands continually brush, keeping time with the rush of his words. He is in excellent physical shape, working out regularly with a personal trainer. His stomach is flat, his chest bulges underneath his shirt, his biceps pushing hard against the sleeves. Between the eruptions of his words, he pauses just long enough to take long swigs from his bottle of Evian water. His voice is a tender tenor, not yet fully polished. His speech is too rapid for best comprehension; there is so much to say and so little time in which to say it! As the speech progresses and intensifies, the pitch of the voice becomes slightly unpleasant, too high, too pinched, too nasal. Elihu has much to learn about the art of public speaking, but his lack of experience does not daunt him in the least. Perhaps some elocution lessons from Eliphaz will add the missing parts to one whose future in the religious arena seems assured.

Yet, with all his physical attributes and his irrepressible enthusiasm and conviction, Elihu finds the appearance of God and God's willingness to speak to Job decidedly depressing and shocking. As Elihu hurries from the stage with the sound of God's voice booming in his ears, his enthusiasm and conviction are both seriously dampened. The look of boyish certainty and the confident cut of his shoulders have both disappeared. And deeper down, Elihu must feel a sense of betrayal; the God whom he has determined to defend against heretics like Job has not acted at all in the way that Elihu has been taught to believe. The speech of God sends Elihu packing, and he retreats in surprised defeat.

Excursus: Readerly Expectations[4]

Before we examine the speeches of God, we should pause and ask the question of expectation: How do we expect God to speak to Job? Of course, I might expect God to speak in one way, while wishing God would speak in another. But the expectations of each reader will certainly affect the way(s) God's speeches are heard.

We first imagine what the various players in the drama expect God to do and say. We can extrapolate these expectations from the substance of their speeches.

Eliphaz would be as amazed as Elihu that God has spoken at all. He has said several times that God "does not trust any of God's servants" (4:18; 15:15) because no human being may ever be righteous before God. God does do "great things," but those deeds are ultimately mysterious and unsearchable (5:9; 22:14). Eliphaz finally concludes from his theology of an untrusting God that God also does not care at all about human behavior, whether bad or good (22:2–3). Yet, in his basic confusion, Eliphaz says over and over that God really does punish the wicked (5:1–14; 15:17–35; 22:12–20). What then does Eliphaz expect from God? If we are to believe his lengthy speeches about the sure fate of the wicked, he can only expect God to hurl a well-aimed lightning bolt at the sinner Job and waste no time with speeches of any kind. For God to tear back the curtains of mystery and speak to a foul sinner like Job would be a most unwelcome surprise to the visionary theologian who thought he alone had a corner on the market of divine communication (4:12–21). God's speech could only be shocking and humiliating to Eliphaz.

Bildad would also be shocked. He has spent nearly all of his words on two certain convictions: The wicked deserve the terrible ends that will surely come to them from God (8:11–19; 18:5–21), and a careful reading of the holy traditions of the past make the first belief absolutely certain (8:8–10). If God would deign to come to Job, God would not talk with him, but would immediately destroy him, as he deserves. The fact that God does not do so would be a terrible surprise for Bildad.

Zophar is the friend most like Elihu. He completely rejects all that Job has claimed about himself and about God (11:2–4), and has warned Job that if God ever would speak, a circumstance he cannot imagine, God would tell him the "secrets of wisdom" (11:6, NRSV), secrets that would reveal definitively that Zophar is right and Job is wrong. But Zophar now hears God speaking to Job, an amazing enough event, but he will also hear that Job has "spoken truth" to God (42:7) while he and his two friends have not. For Zophar, a more surprising outcome to the dialogue could hardly be imagined!

We need add nothing to what we said above about Elihu's expectations.

Job has so many expectations that it is finally difficult to pin him down concerning what he wants from God. But several basic desires are clear.

1. He expects God to vindicate him, to announce to the universe that Job is innocent of any wrongdoing and that the disasters that have befallen him are the result of God's error. That error may be the result of God's maliciousness (9:22–24) or God's confusion (7:12), but the error is surely God's.

2. If Job's lengthy talk of expectations for God in chapter 9 is taken seriously, we might conclude that Job expects God to: ask questions no one can answer (9:3, 15), not really listen to Job's voice (9:16), crush Job with a

"tempest," and generally overwhelm Job with divine power that is unstoppable (9:4–12, 19).

3. If Job's imaginative visions of a third figure are kept in mind, perhaps he hopes that an umpire would level the playing field to enable a genuine dialogue to ensue between Job and God (9:33); or perhaps a great courtroom drama would be played out between God and Job's heavenly witness (16:18–22); or perhaps a final gun battle between God and Job's Avenger would result in the death of God and thus the end of Job's torment (19:23–27). Though each of these wild flights were eventually rejected by Job as impossible, their memory lingers in the drama and could serve as possible expectations of God, if not for Job, then perhaps for some readers.

4. If Job continues to believe that God does indeed reward the righteous and punish the wicked, though he often calls such a belief into the most serious question (see the whole of chapter 22, for example), what he may desire most is the return of his good name as a man of faith and goodness. He wants no longer to be the "laughingstock" of his community, the butt of all their jokes (12:4). He wants God to move him off the ash heap and back into the life he feels he deserves, the life appropriate for a man of exemplary piety and model behavior (see his oath of innocence in chapter 31).

5. Whatever God may say, Job wants God to appear, to come and address Job's pain and frustration. The friends, all four of them, have done nothing to assuage Job's pain. In fact, they have in numerous ways added to that pain with their groundless and cruel accusations and their curt dismissals of his statements. Job may want God to act differently than they have. Deep down, Job would like God to be like God originally was to him, a "beacon light" for his paths and a "guardian" of his life (29:2–3).

Any one of these expectations, or a combination of any or all of them, may be in Job's mind as God's voice thunders from the storm.

I have heard readers offer me various expectations over the two decades in which I have conducted studies of the book of Job with clergy and laity:

1. God needs to treat Job like the "arrogant little creep" (I quote a reader here) that he is. Actually, Job knows no more about the source of his problems than the friends do, so his blasphemous blaming of God is little more than the chirpings of a birdbrained pipsqueak. God needs to tell Job where to get off, to get himself out of the center of the picture of the universe, and to allow God to run things in the way God will, not the way that Job wants. The appropriate stance for any human in the face of God is not brash and absurd questioning, but worship and obedience and acceptance of God's power and control of all things.

2. God should be a lot kinder than those horrible friends! All they wanted to do was destroy Job. They did not care about his pain and suffering, but only worried about the viability of their own theologies. God should demonstrate God's deep love and care for God's lifelong servant, Job, and should tell those friends where to get off. God would not need to say anything at all, but could come in silence and encircle Job with divine loving, showering on him the deep joy of God's presence. Surely, all of Job's terrible and anguished questions would be swallowed up in the radiance of God's self-giving.

3. God should answer Job's questions! Why has all this happened to him? God should admit that the Satan goaded God into the test, and that if God had it do over again, God would have refused to be drawn in by the Satan's wiles. Job is at least partially right; it was nothing he did that brought on the disasters of his life. Yet God needs also to convince Job that God is not the monster Job believes God to be. Nor is God the uncaring being of Eliphaz or the overpowering rewarder and punisher of Bildad, Zophar, and Elihu. God cares deeply for God's creation and is ever in the business of sustaining it in the face of human and natural threat.

4. Perhaps God really is as Job says! When God comes, perhaps God will bluster and blow, prattle on about God's great power, and pay no attention at all to Job's pain or Job's questions. Perhaps the uncaring God of Eliphaz is not as far wrong as we imagined. God may be just as intent as the friends to defend the divine person and honor rather than show genuine care for human pain and confusion.

These four expectations, and variations of them, summarize what some readers expect God to do and say in the divine speeches. It should be noted that some of these expectations say as much, or more, about the reader as they say about the book of Job. So it always is when we read. There can be no such thing as a disinterested reading, a presuppositionless exegesis. When we read, we read ourselves as we read any text. For example, if I want God to be "kinder than those friends," it may be that I have already in my head the notion that the God I know is a kind God; hence, I project onto this God my hopes and expectations. If I am an agnostic about matters theological and have no particular expectations about the actions of a kind God, or any God at all for that matter, I will not project that particular trait onto Job's God, but I may project others from my repertoire of divine thinking: indifference, perhaps, or a lack of ultimate power. The God I actually hear speaking to Job is at least in part a creation of mine, the reader's, as I read the words written by the poet.

And there is another important factor in this question of expectations. By the time the divine speech begins, my emotional connection to the drama will be playing a very important role in my evaluation of God's words. If I am so closely identified with Job as the aggrieved party in the case (see 3 and 4 above), I am very likely to hear the speech of God with specifically Joban ears. But if I am thoroughly disgusted with the arrogance of Job, and with his statements about God, I will hear the speech rather like 1 above; and if I am very uncomfortable about the tenor of the dialogue, the anger and cruelty displayed by Job and all four of his friends, I will likely hear the speech as something far different than angry and cruel. I may be so glad that God has finally come to Job that I care little for what God actually says (see 2 above). In any case, there are intellectual, theological, and emotional expectations all participating in the ways God's words are heard. We all must identify our own expectations as we listen to the divine voice at last speaking to Job.

CHAPTER 7

Job 38—42

Job 38:1—40:5

The narrator introduces God with words that have become very familiar in 38:1. Three things should be noticed about this sentence. First, the poet says it is YHWH who answers, not El or Shaddai or Elohim. This God is the God of Israel, the God who acted and spoke in the prologue. Second, YHWH "answers" Job. The poet announces that in some way what YHWH is about to say is in fact an answer to Job. Whether it is an answer as Job or we might expect, or whether it is an answer to the questions Job or we are asking, is a different matter. Third, YHWH speaks "from the tempest." The only other time this word is used in the Hebrew Bible with this spelling is in Nahum 1:3, where God is described as coming in "tempest and storm." With the use of this word, the poet signals to the reader that Job is about to receive a special visit from God. And from this tempest, YHWH speaks immortal words (vv. 2–4).

The opening words of this speech sound like a salvo from a cannon. We might paraphrase as follows: "Who would be so foolish as to obscure the world's design when they know absolutely nothing about it?" The word translated "design" is often read "counsel," but "design" is what YHWH clearly intends. What Job has challenged is the basic design of the cosmos; he has accused God of mismanagement, of overt cruelty, of allowing the wicked to rest easy and to triumph. These accusations have been made by someone who is "devoid of knowledge," and have served the function of "darkening" or "obscuring" the reality of God's ways in the world. This is the beginning of an answer to Job, as the poet promised, but it is hardly a direct answer to the kinds of questions Job has been asking.

Rather than direct answers, Job receives a challenge from YHWH. You have asked all sorts of questions of me, so now I will ask some questions of you; and you *will* answer these questions. Each of the questions has a simple answer: "nowhere," "I don't know," "only you," "no." From 38:4–38, Job is given a lesson in ancient meteorology: wind and wave, snow and rain, constellations and clouds. The fact of these questions is clear enough, but what is the point of them?

And right here, issues of expectation and emotional engagement with the drama come to the fore. My own initial reading experience of this speech can serve as illustration of the dangers of not paying attention to expectations and emotional involvement. My unpublished 1975 dissertation on irony in Job concluded that Job was right about God. All the fears he expressed in chapter 9 about a meeting with God are ironically confirmed in chapter 38. God comes in a tempest, asks hordes of questions Job cannot begin to answer, and apparently does not listen to Job's voice at all. God is thus a blowhard, more concerned with divine majesty and power than with human suffering and confusion. Job is horribly right about God.

I came to this conclusion because I had so closely identified with Job in my engagement with the drama that the lack of a direct answer from YHWH was intolerable to me. It was grossly unfair and appallingly cruel of YHWH not to pay careful attention to what Job had actually asked and to give attention to some sort of response to that. In a year-long seminar on Job, one of the students concluded that when God made an appearance and spoke like this, the audience would burst out laughing, while Job would wink slyly at them and mouth the words, "I told you so!" I agreed.

I had identified so strongly with the hero that I could hear the drama only with Job's ears. Job's understanding of things had become my understanding of things to the exclusion of all other possible understandings. To be sure, I was led to this identification by the movement of the drama itself. With whom else could I possibly identify when the choices were among the four friends and Job? The four are buffoons, and however unpleasantly arrogant Job may be, he is a remarkable embodiment of pluck and integrity. He can be seen as nothing less than a moral hero, a theologian willing to go to the outer limits of tradition in order to maintain his convictions. He did not fail to call God names that the tradition would only judge blasphemous, but his own experience could lead him nowhere else. In short, Job was for me the very embodiment of the radical, independent theologian, calling into question the traditions of his day, traditions that had become straightjackets from which I needed escape. It was hardly a coincidence that I came to this reading of Job in the midst of the Vietnam War and the Watergate debacle.

But Job's ears are only one pair that may be used to hear God. Other hearings are possible.

1. The very fact that God speaks gives the lie to the claims of the four friends, all of whom were convinced that God would not speak to Job at all or would destroy him if a meeting ever took place. In fact, many commentators have concluded that the most important thing about the speeches of God are not the words but the very fact of God's coming to Job.[1] But why would the poet lavish such long attention on such rich poetry unless we were supposed to read and take seriously the words written? The actual words *are* important.

2. God's tone is harsh; there is scorn and no little sarcasm dripping from the divine mouth. But that is necessary, given the very harsh tone of the speeches of Job himself. God has heard ten very long speeches from Job, many of them brimming with invective for the "monster of the heavens." With each speech Job moves God farther and farther away from the center of the creation and places himself and his concerns more and more directly in that center. The harsh tone not only grabs the attention of the harsh Job but also decenters him, shoves him out of the spotlight of the cosmos. That goal also explains why the meteorological show is conducted; the creation and its sustaining are God's first and most important deeds. No human is involved in any of that (see 38:25–27). Job has given

no thought to these ways of the powerful God. Whence comes the grass? Whence comes the rain that brings the grass, even in uninhabited places, places completely devoid of human life?

But the point for Job is that God must provide for far more in the world than the supposed injustices of one human being. The world simply does not revolve around Job and his special needs, but around God and the complex world that God has created and is in the business of sustaining. And the remainder of this first speech makes that point in another way with a different set of examples.

From 38:39–39:30 God turns to the world's animals to illustrate the sermon to Job. This zoological catalogue reinforces the notion of God's care for a complex world, because once again the emphasis is on creatures who have little or nothing to do with human beings. Indeed, save for the great "war horse" of 39:19–25, none of these creatures has any direct relationship to humanity at all. They are the wild creatures who are cared for by the providential God. Job has never given a single thought to the care and feeding of the raven, for example, but God's sermon says he should do so. Once again, Job is shoved off creation's center and is forced to look more broadly at the whole world of God. And this catalogue of animals leads to a third reason for the tenor of this first speech of God.

3. Job and his friends continued to believe that the world was a very simple place to fathom; the good received good and the bad received bad. Job believed it should be that way, but it was not, while the friends believed it was that way, period. The catalog of animals rejects the belief out of hand. The description of both the ostrich and the raven force us to think quite differently about any supposed easily understood, mechanical universe. The ostrich, with wildly flapping wings that work not at all for flight, the very essence of the bird world, is also a poor parent, says the poet. It "leaves its eggs on the ground, forgetting that a foot might crush them" (39:14–15). This bizarre creature has been so made by YHWH who "has made it forget wisdom" and "has given it no share of understanding" (39:17). With creatures like this one roaming the world of God, how could anyone imagine the world could be easily understood?

And the raven lives on the precarious heights far from the care, even the sight, of any human beings, while "its young gulp blood; where the slain are, there he is, too" (39:30). Even the blood of corpses is somehow a necessary part of God's design, that blood that Job demanded never be forgotten so that he could be vindicated (16:18). Job thought only of spilled innocent human blood, but blood forms more than human witness; it is the very food of some of YHWH's creatures.[2]

And another thing must be noted. Some creatures must necessarily die that others may live; nature really is red in tooth and claw.[3] Are the questions of righteousness and wickedness the right questions to ask when addressing the shape and motion of YHWH's creation? The implied answer of this meteorological and zoological speech is no. The actions of God are not, in fact, centered in conventional responses to wickedness and righteousness. The universe is, in fact, filled to the brim with mystery and surprise and wonder. The theology of Job and the friends provided for none of these. God's answer to Job is: "Think again, Job. Open your eyes wider to the whole of the cosmos. Redirect your attentions away from what you have done to what I am doing."

And YHWH concludes the first speech with a parting and summarizing challenge (40:2). Job has brought suit against God, and God has now offered evidence that suggests that the suit should be thrown out of court due to ignorance. Am I not right, Job, that your understanding of the true design of the universe is faulty, truncated, spotty, and finally false? Can you correct me in this? Can you answer me in this? Job does answer YHWH's extraordinary catalogue of the world's wonders in a most peculiar way. Once again, expectations are important as we listen to Job's answer (40:3–5).

This answer is in the main a capitulation to the overwhelming power of God, but I do not think that Job has actually *heard* God's speech at all. The intentions for the speech that I suggested above have passed over Job's head completely in precisely the same way it passed over my head completely when I first read it. Job is so angry and so furiously disappointed at the tone and the content of YHWH's first address that he can do nothing more than shut up in disgust. His emphatic refusal to speak another word is itself a claim and a kind of refutation. Job's reaction to the speech is as mine first was and as was my classmate's; Job believes he has been proven right by the speech of God from the storm, and his tone here is sarcastic and snide.

It begins with that common Hebrew interjection, "Look," a sharp rejoinder used to call particular attention to a change of scene or to highlight the words about to be spoken. He first says that "he is small," a verb sometimes translated "trifling" or "lightly esteemed." But by far the more common reading is "cursed." In fact, it was this verb that began the entire dialogue when "Job opened his mouth and cursed his day"(3:1). Perhaps Job means both things here; he feels not only small and trifling but also cursed. God and the four friends have again and again cursed him, and he has never denied that in the face of the power of God he is certainly small.

He then adds, "How can I disagree," or more literally, "What [or "how"] can I answer you?" There are quite literally no answers for any of YHWH's questions, and Job has no intention of giving any. This fact does fulfill what Job predicted in 9:3; if God ever deigned to come, "one could not answer him once in a thousand times." And so it is, cries Job with a wink; how could anyone answer such questions?

And he proceeds to put his hand on his mouth. This gesture is mentioned at two other places in the book (29:9; 21:5). The prophet Micah employs the phrase to describe what the nations of the earth will be forced to do when the God of Israel performs wonders; "they will lay their hands on their mouths" (Mic. 7:16). The gesture is not merely a sign of silence; it is also a recognition that something terrible has occurred and that the only possible response to the terror is silence. What Job implies here is that the terrible God of his worst nightmares has appeared, and he must clap his hand over his mouth in horror at the sight.

Verse 40:5 is merely a statement of future intention after verse 4's announcement of present reality as Job sees it. He has spoken, and at great length, earlier, but he has come to the end of his answering. God is bigger and stronger than Job and will not listen to him or answer his concerns. As far as Job is concerned, the drama must end here. God has won, just as Job always feared God would, but for the reader such a victory is surely a hollow one. Job is silenced, but his concerns remain apparently unexamined and unanswered. Such an ending as this is deeply unsatisfying. And it is also deeply unsatisfying to God, because God launches immediately into another speech, and a quite different speech.

Comment

God's first speech must be judged a failure, because it does not offer any sort of satisfactory conclusion to the drama. This is so for the following reasons:

1. Job cannot hear God's speech, because it is couched in language designed to alienate the sufferer rather than to invite him to listen. I suggested above that God intends the speech to announce that God *will* speak to those who cry out, despite what the traditional theologians want to say, that Job needs to get himself off the center of creation in order that he might see more of the fullness of the divine creation, and that that creation is far more mysterious and complex than the mechanical view of it can begin to appreciate. But none of these intentions can be heard, because the mode of their presentation is not listenable by the great and anguished sufferer. He wants answers to his questions, not meteorological and zoological descriptions. However much God would like for Job to comprehend the indirect niceties of the divine answers to him, Job is in no mood to appreciate God's poetic subtleties. In short, Job shuts God's words out, hearing in them only reprimand and bluster. God preaches a poor sermon, not because of poor content but because of poor style. God simply does not take with any seriousness the receptive position of the divine audience. Like too many modern preachers, God does not pay careful enough attention to the context and audience of the address, and consequently it falls on unwilling ears.

2. The reason that Job could not hear the real intentions of God's speech is that he hears no new vision of God in

the speech. For him, the God of this first speech is precisely the God he predicted in chapter 9. In fact, this God seems little different from the God predicted by Zophar and Elihu, a God given over to the wonders and mysteries of the cosmos, but a God reluctant to come clean about any of that to a sinner like Job (see 11:5–6 and 37:15–18 for two examples). Still, God thinks God *has* come clean, but because Job is not yet ready to hear, does not hear. Job hears from God what Job has heard from the friends, a refusal to listen, a refusal to provide substantial answers to his substantial questions.

The reader is urged to a close identity with Job and is made very anxious for an appearance of God to untangle the knots of the dialogue and to bring the agonizing experience of the sufferer to a good end. But the God who comes does not meet any of Job's expectations and thus does not meet many of ours. Only those readers who wish God to put Job in his place can be fully satisfied with this first divine address. The rest of us are left to gnash our teeth or to shut our disappointed mouths or to long for something else. It is that "something else," I believe, that the poet finally provides.

3. I sense that God is also disappointed in God's own performance in the first speech. God's parade of wonders did not at all accomplish what God had in mind. If God thought that such a catalogue would satisfy the hungry Job, Job's sullen and sarcastic response and sharp vow of future silence must surely have brought God up short. Job cannot, will not, hear such things said in such a way. And so God speaks again, because God *must* speak again. Nothing really has been resolved by this first speech.

Job 40:6—41:34

God begins the second speech by repeating a line verbatim from the first; 40:7 is identical to 38:3. However, 38:2, the claim that Job had "darkened the design of God with words devoid of knowledge," is not repeated. That lack of repetition signals a different content. God will refer again to the design of the creation, but Job is not charged this time with obscuring that design; rather, YHWH charges Job with something much more direct, eschewing the indirect rhetoric of the first address. After the repeated challenge of 40:7, God asks two questions in verse 8.

This is a very important sentence in the argument of God with Job. Job in 27:2 had accused God of "turning aside" his "justice." Now YHWH accuses Job of wanting to shatter YHWH's "justice." Job has desired for most of the dialogue to meet God in a courtroom where Job's personal justice could find vindication. Those claims for personal justice have had the effect of shattering God's justice, a justice that can only be understood on a far higher plane than Job has thus far been able to understand. YHWH's justice has much more to do with order than it has to do with a mechanical morality. Job's question of personal justice is seen finally for what it is: quite beside the point of the actual workings of the world of God. And by implication the friends' beliefs are also quite beside the point.

With Job's ultimate irrelevance established, now YHWH can ask the very personal question: Do you have to make me wrong so that you can be right? Is this the only alternative in the universe? This is, of course, a direct challenge to the claim made by Job in 27:5, "Far be it from me to say that you are right; as long as I have breath in me, I will never push aside my integrity." So YHWH now asks if that is the only way to formulate the problem of the pain of the universe: If I am righteous, then God must be wicked. Precisely at that point Job and his four friends have badly missed the mark. A search for individualized justice at the expense of the mysteries and wonders of cosmic order can only lead to inevitable disappointment, frustration, and fury.

Job must raise his sights higher and ask after the ordering of the cosmos. Job has claimed that God should be about the business of "crushing the wicked in their place" (40:12) and "hiding them together in the dust" (40:13). If Job thinks that is what God should do, then Job is asked to do it, to use his El-like arm and deal with the wicked as he thinks God should.

This divine challenge does two very important things. First, it demonstrates the complete absurdity of Job's and the friends' understanding of the actions of God in the world. God does not in fact go about crushing the wicked in their place; Job knows this only too well and says it many times. He *wishes* God would so act, so that he could believe in this mechanical God and get the rewards he then would deserve. But no such God exists or ever did exist. With this little scenario, the theology of the friends collapses like the house of cards it has always been. Second, and following from the first, it undercuts Job's basic challenge that the burden of proof is now on God to demonstrate Job's wickedness or to admit that God is the wicked one. Job's demand that God show him the errors that have brought on the attacks of God is a challenge that is completely off the mark, because the fact is God does not act like that at all. With this remarkable passage, the cord connecting the actions of human beings and the inevitable reactions of God is forever cut. We can no longer think, says the poet, that anything we do will either win God's inevitable favor or earn God's inevitable punishment. With this speech, God's graceful freedom is let loose in the world, and our attempts to control it or manipulate it or coerce it are finally useless.

The tenor of verses 8–14 has often been said to be harsh or unfair; how could a sufferer on an ash heap ever deck himself with the "majesty and glory" of God and do the works of retribution? Thus, these words have often sounded much like those of the first speech, designed to convince him once and for all that he is not God. I hear God in a gentler, more playful mood. The very absurdity of the challenge–"act like you think I act!"–gives rise to a divine chuckle rather than divine sarcasm. I paraphrase the lines: "Job, Job, your attempts to indict me and prove yourself innocent are based on the wrong premises. I do not, repeat, do not, reward the righteous and punish the wicked. If you think I do, then give it a whirl yourself. Go on; I'll wait. But the problem is there are absolutely no models for such behavior. You do not know where to start, and neither do I, because I have never done it either! So, let's talk about something else, OK?" Habel summarizes the point very well.

> If Job can rule the world according to the limited moral law Job administered in his own society, then God will

acknowledge Job as the victor and pay him homage. But as the preceding speech about the "design" of the cosmos and the subsequent portrayals of the chaos monsters also reveal, the world is not run according to the moral principle Job and his friends had espoused. Chaos and evil are part of the world;...Rule according to the wisdom principle leads to balance and freedom; rule according to the principle of retributive justice leads to imbalance and rigidity.[4]

But still the speech cannot end, because the issue of cosmic order has been raised over against the issue of personal retributive justice. God needs to provide Job and the reader with some examples of this cosmic order, examples even more powerful and persuasive than the common ones offered in the first speech. God now turns to the world of mythology to close the discussion with Job and to convince him that the world in which he lives is very different than he imagined it to be, along with the God who made it.

Two great creatures are now discussed at considerable length. They are the great land monster, Behemoth, and the great sea monster, Leviathan. It was common in the early study of the book to think of these two creatures as hippopotamus and crocodile, respectively. Most commentators now see these two creatures for what they are: vast creatures of earlier myth who are not at all to be identified with the animals God pictured for Job in the first speech. Their difference from them is part of the point. By parading these two monsters before the eyes of Job, YHWH ups the ante of the portrayal of the cosmic design. If Behemoth and Leviathan have a place in God's cosmos, then the purpose and shape of that cosmos need to be thought of afresh.

The important point is made at the very start of the introduction of the mighty Behemoth (40:15). Behemoth, a name that means something like "the beast," is a creation of God, not some sort of independent adversary of God, some satanic figure. These two mythic creatures are those symbols of the forces of chaos that are overcome by the high God, Baal in the Canaanite texts, and are examples of even earlier stories of violent creation in Mesopotamia and Egypt.[5] But the important point here is that Behemoth is a creation of YHWH just as much as is Job himself. In fact, the grammar of the sentence could well imply that Job's creation and Behemoth's creation were somehow equivalent events, equally wonderful, equally important.

God does not challenge Job to do anything but look at the beast and learn something of the lesson he failed to learn in the first speech, namely, that evil and chaos exist in the world of God. Somehow, Job must learn that both he and Behemoth have common origins and are therefore bound up together in the world created by YHWH. YHWH will not destroy Behemoth in order that Job may live free in a perfectly ordered and moral world. No, the existence of Behemoth, and his creation by YHWH, suggests that the cosmos is far more mysterious, far more messy, than Job had imagined. He may "eat grass like a cow," but he is no being to be trifled with, given his terrible physical description of verses 16–18. Yes, God is finally able to "take him by the mouth with rings" (40:24), yet no mechanical view of divine action can possibly fit in a universe wherein the fearsome Behemoth finds a place!

And so also Leviathan. Any ancient reader of the book would have known well of this twisting serpent of the sea. Like Behemoth, Leviathan is a symbol of chaos and evil ever ready to rise and devour the world. And also like Behemoth, Leviathan is given a terrifying description, a portrait of invincibility designed to scare any would-be attackers away. Who can hope to take on monsters the likes of these two? Without the power of God vigilant, they could have free reign to destroy. Yet they too, like Job, are creatures who find their places in the complex world of God. They too, like Job, are finally controlled by the commanding power of YHWH, who silences the boasting of Leviathan (41:12) just as Job's boasting was silenced. At the end of Leviathan's long description YHWH proudly points to the serpent and declares, "he is king over all proud children" (41:34). In 28:8 in the poem of wisdom, the author says that no "proud children" have ever found the way to wisdom. These are the only two uses of this phrase "proud children" in the Hebrew Bible. Perhaps Job is the intended referent. Great

Leviathan is king over proud Job, and proud Job cannot ever learn the way to wisdom. Proud Job is being shown again and again that the world and God are not as he supposed.

Comment

So now we can ask why these two beasts have been brought onto the stage at this late juncture in the play. Once again I see multiple reasons.

1. The mode of God's second address is different from the first, the better to capture Job's attention. The second speech begins with very direct attention to what Job has actually asked. It turns out that God has been listening after all. The surprise is that Job's questions are not so much brushed aside, as they were by the friends, but placed in a very different context of cosmic reality that made them ultimately irrelevant to the real world revealed now by YHWH. This was accomplished by YHWH with the ludicrous challenge to Job to act as he thought YHWH acted, which was quite impossible, given the obvious fact that YHWH did not act like that either. Then Behemoth and Leviathan are trotted out in order that Job can see firsthand that chaos and mystery are a definite and real part of God's complex creation and that there is no mechanical escape from that truth. The two beasts are proof positive that God does not destroy the wicked willy-nilly, though God does play a continual role in controlling them, both at the cosmic level and at the human level.

2. The two beasts offer Job much food for thought concerning the basic nature of YHWH. In a world where Behemoth and Leviathan are to be found, any notions that God easily and constantly controls the forces of chaos without struggle are proven false. And with that the notion of simple rewards and punishments becomes quite out of the question. If YHWH is ever in the business of keeping a wary eye on Behemoth and Leviathan, making sure that their destructive natures are not allowed to gain the upper hand, and if YHWH is also in the business of

feeding the ravens and the lions and even the silly ostrich, it is no longer conceivable that God is mechanically ordering the cosmos on the basis of human righteousness and wickedness. This wondrous world of YHWH is far more than a simple world of retribution, but rather a deeply complex and mysterious place. Thus, Job and his friends are called upon to do some large revisioning.

3. Behemoth and Leviathan are also parts of a great story, an ancient tale wherein God creates them but is ever in the process of subduing them as well. YHWH's relationship with them, and with Job, is an ongoing one of struggle and newness. And this ancient tale offers to Job what he so desperately needs from God, namely, a new vision of the Divine and a new vision of his place in the divine cosmos. YHWH plainly does not want the forced capitulation that Job offered after the failed first speech. YHWH, in moving from the natural world of the first speech to the supernatural world of the second, reveals to Job something of what it truly is like to be God of this universe, that it is finally *God's* universe, not at all the one envisioned by Job and his friends. And after YHWH makes light of Job's absurd notion of the ways in which God governs the universe, YHWH shows Job something of what that divine governance really is.

Job has been crying out against the chaos of human life, but how much greater is the chaos with which YHWH strives? This cosmic glimpse by no means answers any of Job's questions, primarily because his questions were not the ones that needed asking. But Job has received a new vision with which to approach his God, a new perspective on the divine reality, and also a new understanding of the world as created by this God. Human suffering is but a part of the chaos that constantly works against God, with which God is in eternal battle. God, in short, has been, and is, engaged in the same struggle as Job, the struggle against chaos, and like Job, God refuses to relinquish that struggle, no matter how often Behemoth and Leviathan rear their hideous heads.

4. This new vision of God also reinterprets the impact of the failed first speech. On the surface, that first speech seemed little different from the angry speeches of the friends, offering Job no new vision of God or the world. But in the light of this second speech, the effect of the first can now be seen to be a description of the universe of God as paradoxically complex, rather than mechanically simple. In God's creation, one finds order, to be sure (38:2–18), rather than Job's claims of chaos (9:22–24); but one also finds humorous incongruity (the foolish ostrich, 39:13–18) and deep mystery (the wasted rain in the uninhabited desert, 38:26). God's world is no easily grasped machine, oiled by retributive justice. "In a world where paradox and incongruity are integral to its design, there is no simplistic answer to the problem of innocent suffering."[6]

Job now has received a new vision of God as YHWH, creator and sustainer as well as struggler with a complex and mysterious order. It is that new vision of YHWH to which Job responds in his famous last speech.

Job 42:1–6

Job's final speech is riddled with thorny problems, in terms of both translation and meaning. I will make only the following observations.

Job is here responding to the accumulated speeches of YHWH. He has received a new vision of God, and every line of his response indicates that fact. Verse 2 does not on its surface represent any new knowledge for Job; he has never denied that God could do whatever God proposed to do. In fact, that was often his problem with God; God's actions were unstoppable and, as far as Job could see, terrible and cruel, given his understanding of God throughout the dialogue. But verses 3–6 put a new face on this belief. Yes, God is active in the world; God's design is operative, but that design is not so easily discerned by humans, and is not easily and simply maintained by God.

Verse 3a is Job's quotation of what he heard God say to him. It is not a direct quotation from 38:2a. There God said, "Who is this who *darkens* the design *with words* without knowledge?" Job paraphrases God to say, "Who is this who *obscures* the design without knowledge?" By paraphrasing in this way, Job focuses attention on what he feels has been his basic problem revealed to him by the speeches of God, namely his lack of knowledge. It has been his words that have revealed that lack, as YHWH said in 38:2a, but Job wants his response to YHWH to be based on his central lack of true knowledge about YHWH. His answer is that he "spoke without discernment [*bin*]" about "wonders beyond him that he did not know." "Discernment" is an oft-used word in the drama. A few of the examples will make the point that the search for discernment, for perception, has all been based on false knowledge of YHWH. Job (6:30; 9:11; 13:1; 14:21; 23:5) either claims to discern what God is doing to him or fails to discern just why God is doing it. Likewise, the friends (Eliphaz in 15:9, Bildad in 18:2, Elihu in 32:9; 34:16; 36:29) all claim that they have the right discernment about the true state of the world and that Job's discernment is seriously askew. After the catalog of God's wonders in the first speech and the wondrous mythological beasts of the second speech, Job now realizes that his discernment has been seriously in error. And the reader knows, too, that the friends' vaunted discernment is also completely wrong.

Job paraphrases YHWH again to begin verse 4. YHWH said in 38:3, "Gird up your loins like a hero; I will question you and you will answer me!" Job paraphrases, "Hear now while I speak; I will question you and you will answer me!" Again, the changes are significant. YHWH said to Job to "gird his loins like a hero." Job has acted the part of adversary throughout the dialogue, challenging God over and over to appear and answer Job's charges. When YHWH does appear, YHWH calls for Job to prepare to play the role he thinks he has assumed against God, that of heroic adversary. YHWH's challenge here is not unlike the humorous one YHWH offers Job at the beginning of the second speech to act like the God Job believes God to be (40:9–14). The fact that Job leaves out of his paraphrase any notion that he is hero, or that he is about to take God on in some sort of wrestling match, indicates that Job is a different character after the two speeches of YHWH.

Verses 5–6 are the key to Job's response, and they have generated an extraordinary amount of comment over the years.

1. Job in 5a begins the rejection of his faulty notions of God by saying that his former knowledge was based quite literally on hearsay, or "the hearing of the ear" (NRSV). Job knew what the friends knew, and the dialogue was all based on that sort of knowledge. It is traditional knowledge, long-hallowed and long-repeated. Yet such knowledge always runs the risk of hardening so much as to exclude any new thinking or new experience. Job admits that his own experience of God has called all of that knowledge into question.

2. In 5b Job announces that he has now "seen" YHWH, rather than merely heard about YHWH. This seeing has led more than a few commentators to focus attention on the theophany of God to the near-exclusion of what YHWH said in the theophany. But the fact that Job twice paraphrases YHWH in his response says that Job listened to the words as well as experienced the appearance. Just for YHWH to appear to Job would not have been enough to convince Job to think differently. Job had to know that he had been heard and taken with great seriousness before he could begin to catch a genuinely new vision of YHWH.

3. Verse 6 is amazingly ambiguous for a valedictory sentence from our hero. The following translations (among others) are all possible:

A. Therefore I reject,
   and I repent on dust and ashes.

B. Therefore I melt;
   and I am sorry on dust and ashes.

C. Therefore I retract,
   and I am sorry for frail humanity.

Each of these three has numerous permutations, and I could add further possibilities. (I do think that the

NRSV's "Therefore I despise myself" is plainly impossible grammatically.) The way one translates the line is of course dependent on the ways one has heard the drama begin its denouement. Once again, we are faced with the question of expectation.

My reading is based on what I think Job is doing in response to the speeches of YHWH. First, he is retracting what he said, because he has just admitted that he did not know what he was talking about. The verb "retract" frequently occurs with a direct object, but there is none here. What Job is announcing is that all of the terrible things he said about God are now seen, in the light of God's visit, to be absurdly false. He retracts all the false claims he made about God during the course of the dialogue. I do not include in the retraction either the great passion with which Job's words were expressed or the blunt repudiations Job offered to the cruel speeches of the friends. He has no intention of repudiating those things.

Job's final words, "I am sorry on dust and ashes," are *not* a repentance in any traditional religious sense. Job here "changes his mind" (see Ex. 32:12, 14; Gen. 6:6), forsaking his position of lamentation and fury on the ash heap. He does not repent at the sight of YHWH, weeping his way to the mourner's bench under the conviction of the divine sermon. He resolves, equipped with the new vision of YHWH offered to him in the theophany, to move away from adversarial complaint and rage toward reconciliation with this God of struggling power and wondrous care for the cosmos. And in the light of this Joban response, YHWH has some further things to say before the drama is to reach its conclusion.

Comment

Job has been changed by the appearance of YHWH. He admits his foolish lack of knowledge, he retracts the astonishing accusations he made against God in the dialogue, and he resolves to change his stance in the drama from one of angry litigant to one of reconciled partner with God. I must repeat again that I do not think Job has repented in the sense that word is often used when speaking of Job's actions. After all, God has not asked him to repent, but to listen and to see something of what God is really like and to think afresh about what this new vision of God could mean. Perhaps such a change could be called "repentance" in the best sense of that word. Job has become a new person for sure, a man ready to enter the world again with a new hope about the universe and a new prospect for his place in that universe. He has rejected his old view of God and is groping toward a new one, and he has given up his rage once he discovered that the rage was directed toward a God who did not exist.

Some would like the drama to end here, but I do not think it can. If Job has become new, we must see him act out of his newness to discover if that newness is genuine. How will he act toward his old and bitter adversaries, the friends? How will he find his way back into his former community? We cannot allow the camera to pull back in a long shot with Job waving from his ash heap while YHWH retreats in the storm! We need to see Job back in the world again.

Job 42:7–17

The epilogue of this play has caused readers no end of trouble. Its basic problem is that it appears to completely upset the great truth that the preceding forty-two chapters have claimed to establish: The world is not established on the basis of retributive justice. Unfortunately, the epilogue seems to do just that! Job is restored to the world, given back double everything he has lost, and lives to a ripe old age of 140, dandling his great-grandchildren on his aged knees. Many commentators have simply deleted the whole thing. However, I think a reading can be given of the epilogue that does not compromise the hard-won truths of the poem.

It must first be recognized that the epilogue actually possesses two scenes that need to be examined separately.

Scene I–Job 42:7–9. The three friends (Elihu is not mentioned at all), whom we saw disappear from the stage under the Joban onslaught, are summarily commanded to appear before YHWH. Not only has YHWH appeared to the disgusting

Job, but now YHWH is about to speak furious words to these three who thought they were YHWH's staunchest and most knowledgeable defenders. The reason for God's anger is that they, unlike YHWH's servant Job (how the word "servant" must have grated on their ears!), "have not spoken the truth to me." "The truth" is quite simply what is correct, what is fully consistent with fact.

Habel well summarizes what this means for our drama.

> Now YHWH's answer announces that Job's bold assertions in the dialogue speeches were likewise free from blame in spite of some rather vitriolic (such understatement!) moments (e.g., 16:9ff). The blunt and forthright accusations of Job from the depths of his agony are closer to the truth than the conventional unquestioning pronouncements of the friends...Job's answers correspond with reality. They are devoid of dissembling and flattery, a trait against which Job warned the friends (23:7–12).[7]

It should not be thought that the truth to which YHWH refers is Job's appraisal of God and God's actions in the world. That cannot be the content of the word "truth," since Job has just repudiated those statements in his final address of 42:1–6. What God affirms as true is Job's integrity, his unwillingness to pretend that the world he saw was somehow not the world in which he lived. This incongruity was the problem of the friends: They saw what Job saw, but they persisted in the falsehood that it just could not be so, given their erroneous and unproven claims about God and that world. It is only Job who spoke truly in the dialogue, because to the very end his integrity remained intact; he could never admit that the friends were right in the face of what his own experience continued to teach him (27:5).

I have translated "truth to God" rather than the more common "truth about God" or "of God." The Hebrew preposition speaks most commonly of direction; another preposition would be used if "about" were the intention. Thus, YHWH appears to mean simply the words that were directed to God by Job were judged to be truly spoken.

Now, in a delightful and ironic about-face, it is the friends who are commanded by YHWH to sacrifice on their own behalf in the presence of Job, YHWH's servant, who now plays for them a kind of priestly role, because he has found the "favor" of YHWH (the common phrase used twice is literally "lifted the face of"). This action is a reversal of Job's actions in the prologue. There he sacrificed untold numbers of fatted beasts on behalf of his ten children, for fear they might have committed some secret sin. This compulsive sacrificing was a signal that Job's relationship with YHWH was based on a kind of terror, rather than a healthy desire to give his best for YHWH. In response, YHWH commands that the friends sacrifice by and for themselves. This very specific and directed sacrificial act is sharply contrasted to the almost desperate and excessive sacrificing Job performed in the prologue. Could the friends' sacrifice in Job's presence not be a rebuke for the hero and an announcement that sacrifice should be done only at YHWH's express command, rather than as a fevered attempt to ward off the assaults of a retributive deity? (One might see a similar notion in the remarkable Ps. 50.) Now that we have been shown that such a deity does not exist, sacrifice can no longer be seen as propitiation, the price for a safe existence.

YHWH then tells the friends that "Job will pray for you." One can almost hear the loud laughter in the audience as the astonished friends bow their heads while Job offers up prayer to God for them! I picture the three, eyes not firmly closed, glancing at one another in bewilderment, incredulous that the disgusting Job has somehow become their priest. They are apparently in need of prayer from this one whom YHWH favors, because YHWH does not favor these three who did not speak truth.

But we should note something important in connection with the scene: There is no hint of retribution here, or reward for anything anyone has done. It does not say that Job is favored *because* he repented. It does not say that the friends should sacrifice to YHWH *in order that* they might find their way back into YHWH's good graces. It does not say that Job should pray for them *in order that* YHWH receive them back. YHWH commands their various actions, and YHWH's will is obeyed.

Job once again plays the role he said he had before the terrible disasters occurred, but he plays that role as a free gift of YHWH, not as reward for his repentance or his truth-telling. The words of the text specifically rule out any hint of reward and punishment.

Can the same be said for the second scene, the closing words of the drama (Scene II, 42:10–17)? The important answer appears in verse 10. The key word is "when." Does the narrator mean that YHWH restored Job's fortunes *because* Job prayed? Or does the sentence imply that there is a temporal connection between Job's prayer and the return of his things? I believe that here there is no connection between Job's prayer and YHWH's restoration. I take the temporal clause quite literally; YHWH restored Job's fortunes *when* he prayed, but that "when" implies nothing about YHWH's reward. I see no necessary connection in this text between the actions of Job and the actions of YHWH. YHWH's restoration of Job is pure gift, not reward.

But that restoration is not simply a return to the beginning of the drama. Job is not all that has changed; his new world from YHWH is indeed new.

1. The restored community first shares a communal meal, a sign of renewed unity and hope (v. 11).
2. "They condoled and comforted him for all the evil that YHWH had brought on him." His brothers and sisters and all his former acquaintances do what those three friends originally came to accomplish, but so miserably failed to do: "condole and comfort him" (2:11). But they are able to do this because they recognize the truth that Job has established and that YHWH has admitted: YHWH brought the evil on Job. The baldness of this statement is stunning, but important. There is evil in the complex design of YHWH's creation, and YHWH is certainly somehow involved in it. Until that fact is understood and accepted, Job cannot do anything but rail against an undeserved fate, and the friends can do nothing else except defend God as the high lord protector of some mechanized universe. Consolation and comfort can only arise when no one is in the business of defending a

pure and simple cosmos from the constant intrusions of the realities of innocent pain and suffering. These folk who are sharing Job's table know well that evil is an inevitable part of the world of God, and rather than defend a world that does not exist, they busy themselves with the comfort of one who has suffered appallingly in that real world. Unlike the three friends, they are real friends to Job, rather than trying to prove him somehow wrong.

3. YHWH's gifts to Job are a blessing. Especially marvelous are his children, once again seven sons and three daughters. But here the narrator shows us that the world of Job is very different now, because the three daughters, rather than those seven sons, get names and are given a piece of the patriarchal inheritance equal to the ones given to the sons.

One tradition in Israel (Num. 27:1–8) says that daughters could only inherit their father's property if there was no male heir. But in the new world of Job, he acts in full justice toward his daughters as he said he had always acted in his patriarchal community (see chap. 31). In the new world of Job, the new vision of God is shining so as to extend the hope and possibility of God's work toward shalom to all God's human creatures, whether female or male.

4. Job dies "full of days," the gift of God extending to twice the traditional "threescore and ten," to 140 years. Like Abraham before him (Gen. 25:8) Job died, old and sated with days. He is thereby connected to the ancient patriarchs, a great and wonderful man, who suffered, who received a visit from YHWH, and who received great gifts from YHWH. Abraham, Isaac, Jacob, and Joseph each suffered, was visited by YHWH, and received great gifts from YHWH. Job is securely one of their number. However, the reason for his memory is in many ways far different from theirs.

Job is the truth-teller, the astonishing man of complete integrity, who, when faced with the worst that the cosmos could throw at him, stood erect and demanded an audience with God.

And so he received the audience, but the God who came was not like the God he expected. And from that visit Job became new, just as much as God became new for him and for us, the readers of the drama. No, it is hardly for his "patience" that Job should be remembered. It is for his truth, his often brutal honesty, his unalloyed integrity, that this man will live in human memory as long as there are humans who question the way of things, who refuse to repeat old thoughts merely because they are old and accepted, who refuse to keep silent while the suffering of the world remains so real. We preachers and those who listen to us could learn much from this man, and in the next chapter we will try to do just that.

CHAPTER 8

"Troubling Physicians Are You All": On Becoming a Joban Preacher

The collectors of the Revised Common Lectionary have a neat solution for the would-be preacher of the book of Job. In four successive Sundays in year B—during "ordinary time" of course—the preacher is given the opportunity to tackle Job. She is to use the prologue (chaps. 1–2) on Sunday 1, one speech of Job's from chapter 23 on Sunday 2, a bit of God's first speech on Sunday 3 (chap. 38), and Job's final response and his restoration by God on Sunday 4. To reduce Job to this sort of Reader's Digest version is sure to distort its meaning and to tame its anger effectively enough to make its impact minimal and those summer Sundays appropriately innocuous. Best stick with the gospel reading, I suppose. But, still, what is one to do with the book? Now that we have read through the whole drama, what can we do with it as preachers and listeners?

I want to see how Job can help us to think about a very large question, namely, What kind of preachers do we want to be after we have grown up? That is, how can Job help us to examine the very stuff of our preaching, its central thrust, its mature awareness of a world of complexity and pain? In short, I think Job challenges us to become more mature preachers and listeners, more aware preachers and listeners. I propose to learn from Job by listening again to him with great care.

Plasterers of Lies and Troubling Physicians

When Job utters these angry and mocking words to his so-called friends, he is in the middle of one of his longest speeches,

149

comprising no fewer than seventy-five verses. This particular phrase can be found amidst the speech in 13:1–5. Quite obviously, Job is thoroughly rejecting something that the friends have been saying to him, and doing so with wildly intemperate words. But just what is it that has him all riled up here? What, more exactly, is the "all" he claims to have seen, and whatever is it that his ear has heard in verse 1?

The answer is to be found in Job's own painful hymn to the destructive power of God in the preceding chapter 12, most especially in verses 14–25 (see my comments on this section in the commentary). Job sings there of the great power of God, but the manifestations of that power are most disconcerting. In a devastating parody of a traditional Israelite hymn, Job's use of the verbs that describe the actions of God to him are difficult to hear. Precisely these are the ways of the God we are discussing, says Job. Hardly a doxology one would hope to sing next Sunday!

Now, it is too simple to conclude that the friends merely disagree with Job on this matter. Of course, they find his evaluations of God and of them to be little less than disgusting atheism, words of no wit or wisdom, uttered by the foulest of sinners. That goes without saying. But the issue drawn by Job is more subtle and more important for us preachers. The elementary lesson at issue is: All created things can teach us that whatever is done is done by God. Job claims that the friends have been saying that he, Job, refuses to learn this elementary lesson. If he would learn it, he could be reconciled to the hand that God has dealt him. In essence, what they have been saying might be put as follows: "All this, my dear Job, is God's doing. Your suffering—and it does indeed look painful, we know—is nothing but a natural, inevitable, ordered, prescribed, intelligible, rational, and coherent part of the 'all' you so scornfully mock." With the astonishing naïveté of Voltaire's Dr. Pangloss, the friends gaze at the complex, mysterious, wayward, peculiar world in which they live and proclaim, "This is the best of all possible worlds!" One imagines they would continue to say this even if confronted by a woman with her right buttock partially bitten off by a rampaging monkey, as Dr. Pangloss himself was able to do.[1]

But we might stop and ask at this point: Why are Job and his poet and I so cynical about such an attitude? Is there not in all of us religious types the call to proclaim order in the face of chaos, to announce the ultimate victory of love in the face of overwhelming hate, to share the promise of a God who brings life out of the very jaws of death? Just what is wrong with these friends' convictions that Job's way of viewing things, namely that God has rejected him arbitrarily, that God hates him, that God has a hidden dark purpose for the creation, is painfully in error? It is hardly as if no other persons since these friends have ever had such notions! Like Dr. Pangloss, who keeps reappearing after several hangings and bludgeonings, after being drawn and quartered, after being decisively done in in any number of ways, so do these attitudes of the friends come back again and again and again. Yes, there are difficulties in the world, but things are not so bad; yes, there is a considerable amount of suffering around, but it could be worse; yes, there is more than enough misery to go around, but it is surely better than it used to be. There are contemporary racist attitudes, but think of the 1950s! There is still a great glass ceiling for women, but remember the 1950s! Homophobia is rampant, but remember the 1950s! "Every day in every way, things are a little bit better" is not a slogan I only remember from the 1950s! The friends find their echoes down through the ages right into the present.

But, I repeat, What's wrong with a little optimism? What's wrong with looking at the glass and triumphantly proclaiming that it really is half-full and is filling up as we look at it? What's wrong with looking at old cynical Job, waving an airy hand at the world, and saying, "Buck up, old boy; God's in God's heaven and all really is right with the world?" I think it comes down to this for Job and for us. What Job has encountered in his own life and experience is an untidy world, not an intelligible one, an arbitrary world, not an ordered one, a cruel world, not a loving one. It is a world where a just person can and does become a joke. Read 12:4.

For Eliphaz, for Bildad, and for Zophar, as well as for Dr. Pangloss, for Norman Vincent Peale, for Robert Schuller, and, yes, for many of us who are comfortable, satisfied, and content, the garden we see is lovely, all things neatly in their place, all places neatly arranged by a beneficent designer who is in all things to be praised. But for Job, and for billions of his heirs throughout the history of humanity on the earth, the garden is often choked with weeds, and nature is red in tooth and claw. David Clines summarizes the point like this: "For the friends the wisdom of the ages has been melted down into a cliché, a saying for all seasons, 'Yahweh's hand has done this'; for Job raw experience, not mulled theology, is true wisdom."[2]

There it is. For Job, raw experience, not mulled theology, is true wisdom. I believe that this dichotomy—experience on the one hand and mulled theology on the other—mirrors our most contentious, contemporary theological debates. It comes down to the question of authority, does it not? Is my own raw experience, or the raw experiences of others quite unlike me, of value for the doing of theology, for the preaching of the word, or are the results of a mulled theology, one handed down, one given to me, the only adequate sources for the task? This is the way that the issue is drawn between Job and his friends; if they are right, then Job's experience is useless as the basis for his beliefs and demands. But if he is right, then the friends are little better than cruel buffoons, cliché-ridden liars, or in Job's trenchant phrase, "troubling physicians."

One need not be a very sophisticated exegete to discern on which side of this stark dichotomy the sympathies of the poet of Job lie. The book's very structure makes the point. The dialogue between Job and friends begins with the pattern of Job–Eliphaz–Job–Bildad–Job–Zophar–Job. Both the first and second cycles of speeches adhere to that pattern. But cycle three brings some startling changes. Eliphaz–Job–Bildad–Job appears, but the speech of Bildad is a mere six verses long, ending in the mordant claim that human beings are but maggots and worms, while there is no speech of Zophar whatever. There have certainly been some disruptions in these speeches by later editors, but the trend is clear enough. The friends have not only not proven Job to be in error; they have themselves been reduced to despairing clichés and silence. Job's own sarcastic claim that their silence is their wisdom in 13:5 is played out in the drama of the dialogue. They say no more after chapter 25 (save, of course, their blustery companion Elihu) until they are attacked by God for their "wrong-speaking" in chapter 42. The poet makes it clear enough that the views of these friends, all four of them, have little genuine value. But is our only option to side with Job uncritically and agree with him that the universe is mismanaged by a moral midget who has it in for the poor creatures who live in it? That can hardly be the text of next Sunday's sermon!

A Different Way to Frame the Question?

Does the poet finally think that Job is right? Are the friends simply wrong while Job is simply right? To conclude so is to miss one of the poet's basic claims. Even though the author has set up the dichotomy I described above between Job and his friends (that is, that either one or the other is right), I think that the dichotomy is judged overly simplistic by its own creator. The poet wants us to probe more deeply into the implications of this simplistic dichotomy to enable us, along with Job, to begin to discover what lies, more importantly, at stake in this remarkable book. And if we follow the poet's lead, we may find equally important clues for our work as preachers. The trail of this deeper meaning begins back in the passage I began with, 13:1–5.

After Job announces to the friends that he is hardly ignorant of the ways of God, as they claim—indeed he is all too conversant with the destructive acts of the deity—he accuses them of being "plasterers of lies" and hence "troubling physicians."

Job is saying that his friends are trying to put a false face on the real truth of things; they are in effect denying the undeniable truth of what Job has experienced as a divine malignancy in the universe by their continuous repetition of theological platitudes. To put it more directly, they simply will not listen to Job's experience. They cannot listen, precisely because that experience is not compatible with their theological platitudes. But though the poet here has once again obviously pitted Job against the friends, the way in which the argument is formulated offers us food for further reflection about our maturity as preachers.

Job's specific accusations here should give us modern preachers pause. In what ways have we been "plasterers of lies" when we have preached? How have we rolled our thin veneers of the gospel over this cankerous world, attempting to plaster over the pains of those we have not heard as we ladled out our platitudes learned in seminary however long ago? How have we become then examples of Job's next figure—"troubling physicians"? Once again, the image is suggestive. The friends from the beginning have claimed to be healers. Eliphaz began his first speech to the furious Job with an attempt to heal the anger and impatience Job poured out in his monologue of chapter 3. He reminds Job that he, Job, used to advise others when they were in trouble, but now that it has come to him he has become so wrapped up in his own concerns that he can no longer hear the wisdom of his own earlier advice. Both Bildad and Zophar fancy themselves to be healers of Job as well, however more authoritarian their means are for doing so.

But Job will have none of such supposed healing. Physicians like you are "worthless," he says. He uses a harsh word here. It is a word most often in the Hebrew Bible connected to false gods. Most especially Isaiah 2 in four places uses the word to pillory gods of silver and gold and those who are foolish enough to follow such non-gods. Psalms 96 and 97 have similar references. By employing this particular word, Job connects the so-called healing ministrations of the friends to its opposite. They are not healing Job with their words; they are rather wounding him, and in the long run killing him with their lies.

Again, we modern preachers are brought up short. How are our attempts to provide healing to a sick world turned into attacks rather than healing, wounds rather than sutures, blows not blessings? The friends' healing consists in their attempts to make Job conform to their way of thinking. Because they have all the right answers, as well as all the right ways to get to those right answers, Job need only come into conformity with them and he will find healing. But Job must reject such healing precisely because his raw experience speaks to him a different truth. The friends' answers can never be more than partial, because they have no way to include within their formulations of the truth a crucial fact—the fact of Job's experience. For them, Job's experience is ruled out by definition and can play for them no role as they attempt to mediate the truth of God as they claim to know it. How have we modern preachers ruled out of our formulations of the truth of God experiences we do not know or refuse to know? How often are our truth formulations like those of the friends, neat, coherent, winsome, clever, but finally painfully limited to our own narrow tradition and our own narrow formualtions of that tradition? What essentially is wrong with such formulations, and why does Job so angrily reject the attempted healing ministry of the friends?

Job's direct attack on the friends as "plasterers of lies" and "worthless physicians" becomes more than just a schoolyard taunt. His accusation means much more than a simple "I'm right and you're wrong." The friends' wrongness primarily consists in their inability to hear Job's pain, his raw experience, and to include that experience in their understanding of the way things really are. What is ultimately wrong with the friends' formulations is that Job simply does not exist for them; his very life has no effect whatever on their understandings of the world or themselves. It is that fact that makes them "plasterers of lies"; their world does most certainly include Job and his raw experience, no matter how inconvenient or untidy that experience may be for their neat and clean conceptions of the way things are.

And so it is for us preachers. No matter how comfortable we get in our proclamations, no matter how coherent we strive to make our statements of faith, no matter how much we would like our pulpits to be places of safety and sanity, the raw experience of the world bombards our souls and cries out for inclusion into our thinking and our feeling. Job will not be silenced even by the most clever and slick of pulpiteers. Christine Smith urges on us preachers what she calls a "ministry of resistance." She uses the word "resistance" in the same way I am, urging us to include the "raw experience" of the world in our preaching. She further suggests that we need to face two primary challenges: (1) to reflect critically on every aspect of our own theology in order to discern those ways in which it perpetuates and undergirds oppression in whatever form that oppression presents itself, through the various exclusions we practice and affirm; and (2) to listen constantly to voices of critique and struggle outside one's cultural and social reality in order to expand and transform one's own homiletical agenda and one's preaching voice.[3] Listening to our Jobs, those who cry out for justice out of their pain and suffering, is something we must do if we are to become Joban preachers, fully mature in our proclamation of the good news.

Growing up Homiletically

It is also here in chapter 13 that Job first makes it clear to the reader and to himself that he can get no ultimate help from these friends. He knows all that they know, but more importantly, his experience of what he knows is so different from theirs that he recognizes they are incapable of hearing him, of really listening to him. That is why he so defiantly turns away from them and toward God in verse 3.

> But I will speak to Shaddai!
> I will argue with God!

As the dialogue progresses, Job more and more will utter defiant words like these, words that do not at all imply that he expects some sort of divine mercy or forgiveness. To the contrary, what Job wants is vindication from God. He has been done a great injustice, and he wants the wrong righted. He can see that these friends have no intention nor the capability to offer such vindication, so he turns away from them in his search. To be sure, they lock horns again and again after this speech, but Job is now clear that his debate with them is effectively over. He must struggle with God directly if he is to find vindication.

But, as he turns away from his bilious friends, he offers them some free words of advice and warning. It is in these words that we preachers can hear some important words for our own tasks today (see 13:7–12).

God will not be happy to discover, after the careful divine examination of verse 9, that those most attempting to justify God's ways to Job in fact resorted to lies to keep God in the clear. Any theology that does not take Job's particular experience into account (i.e., a righteous man who has become a joke) is quite simply a lie. Lies, for whatever reason, should never be spoken about God. The four lines of rhetorical questions (vv. 8–9) are an expression of Job's amazement and horror that anyone could resort to lies in the service of truth. And right here we find the basic message we maturing preachers need to hear from the book of Job. If we want to become Joban preachers, we must in all things be purveyors of truth, even and especially if that truth is the painful and inexplicable experience of Job, the righteous one who has become a joke.

Neither Job nor I am suggesting that any preacher purposely sets out to lie. We pride ourselves on our biblical exegesis, our careful attention to the pulse of our congregations, our careful concern for the experiences the wider world presents, our sensitive listening to the vast reaches of our own inner lives. Our training stands with us as we present the word we are given.

But Job warns us there is a danger of lying here nonetheless. And the danger comes precisely at the point of our very calling to speak for God. To speak for God is often to speak in defense of God, to justify God's ways to humanity. But, warns Job, genuinely to speak for God is at the same time to open oneself up to divine scrutiny. To take up God's cause is to make one liable to God's evaluation. Thus, the friends are in a dangerous spot, and so are we. A defense of God can more safely be undertaken by taking the stance of a detached observer of the ways of God. This is exactly what Job accuses them of doing.

How much easier and safer it is, says Job, to speak on God's behalf from the comfortable position of theological certitude, from tightly structured, long-hallowed notions of moral and intellectual rectitude, from the established and acceptable role of respected arbiter of religious taste. Such a position is insulated from life and its experience, and, ultimately for Job, then insulated from a fresh confrontation with God. Job here does not speak of a confrontation with the several notions about God but a confrontation with the living God, a God as much shrouded in mystery as easily seen and appropriated. Job's call for a meeting with this God brings us preachers to ask with him: Just what sort of God is it that we think we are proclaiming?

Job's God

And now we arrive at the ultimate question of theology. Just who is this God Job would have us preachers meet? What finally shocks Job about the theological position of the friends, that carefully wrought traditional position that has God oh-so-well figured out, is its ready willingness to shrink from mystery and calmly purport to justify the ways of God to humanity. It is all so neat and clean. God is signed, sealed, and delivered, boxed up, dusted off during holiday times, displayed for appropriate praise and then returned to the shelf to await another showing. God is a sort of yardstick, always the same length, who is laid against the world to see if the world measures right. Anything less or more than thirty-six inches is judged accordingly, found wanting, then lengthened or shortened accordingly. After the procedure is finished, the yardstick is placed back behind the door to await another time of measurement. But one always knows exactly how long the stick is—it never varies at all. The God of the friends is so domesticated, so restrained, so predictable. Job knows of no such God. His raw experience has taught him otherwise.

When Job speaks of God, awe and terror are in his words. We have already heard one of his hymns from chapter 12. Chapters 9 and 16 are other examples.

The God of Job is active, engaged in the life of the world. But more. The actions of this God are not always easy to fathom. Again and again Job will ask his friends and God just what is happening to him. Just how can he, a righteous man, be at the same time a laughingstock to the world, a suffering man who by all theological lights should be living the good life? The friends say, "That's how it is, Job. Ash heaps always come to those who deserve them. You are on yours because the world is like that. You always get what God dishes out, and that's OK. Be reconciled."

I do not intend to trace the history of such a mechanistic view of the universe in Israel, but it is surely exemplified most clearly in what I would call a badly caricatured reading of some passages from the book of Deuteronomy.[4] "Do this and live long," it certainly does say. No matter that the heart of the book may be said to be found in chapter 7, where all human action is a response to the love of the God who first chose Israel and saved it from the bondage of Egyptian slavery; persons in every age since have reduced the idea to the simple one of Job's friends, the notion of automatic reward and punishment.

This caricatured idea of God is easy enough to lampoon, and Job's poet is the classic lampooner. But what about Job's idea of God? Where does this wild God of mystery and terror and surprise come from in the tradition? Once again, I will not provide anything like a full review, but its roots are deep and wide in the soil of Israel, and we would do well to remember them if we are to avoid proclaiming the God of the friends, who is ever attractive and safe to us.[5]

I wish to address two passages from the older traditions to suggest that the God of Job's experience is well known in Israel. By far the more familiar of the two is found in Genesis 18:22–32. Abraham and Sarah have both laughed in the face of the ridiculous promise of God that the prune-faced couple will have their own son, notwithstanding their obvious physical liabilities that serve to make such a prospect highly unlikely. Right after Sarah has had a silent chortle in response to still another reiteration of this foolish prediction, Abraham finds himself toe-to-toe with God. He soon discovers that God is about to practice a little urban renewal in and around the thriving suburbs of Sodom and Gomorrah, and that this project will be a bit more than a block-by-block trash cleansing. Abraham reacts to the news with horror (vv. 23–25).

God has determined to destroy the evil cities, but Abraham raises the crucial question of justice. Are wicked and righteous to be treated the same? In the world of God are there to be no distinctions between wicked and righteous? As we saw, this is a palpably Joban question. Abraham answers, "God will surely not treat righteous as wicked," and in this story God indeed does not do so. Job answers, "God does exactly treat righteous as wicked," and his own experience makes the case. The fact, however, that Abraham raises the issue at all in the story suggests that it is a lively concern in the tradition.

The second passage makes that concern certain. I wish to focus on the single verse 1 Samuel 3:18 as a part of the much longer story of Samuel, Saul, and David. The verse is a speech by the old priest of Israel, Eli, uttered after his student, the youthful Samuel, has been called by God in the temple to tell his teacher that God has turned away from him and has given new authority to Samuel. Samuel reluctantly speaks this harsh word to his mentor only after Eli demands that he withhold nothing of the divine oracle from him. That brings us to Eli's response, which is wonderfully ambiguous. It could be read, "It is Yahweh. Let him do whatever is good for him to do"; that is, Eli may be acquiescing to the divine will, though that will would depose him from his place of power. One could hear it as a full trust in the power of God to act well in all things. However, the phrase could also be read, "YHWH will do whatever YHWH wants to do." Again, Eli could be acquiescing to YHWH's will, or he could be wearily giving in to the overwhelming and unpredictable power of YHWH, who always does whatever YHWH chooses to do. If the latter reading is given, Eli could be said to agree with the earlier song of Hannah, Samuel's mother, which she sang in response to the gift of her son to her in her old age (1 Sam. 2:6–8).

Both Hannah and Eli record from their experiences what Job knows from his own raw experience, namely, that there is both power and mystery in God, for this is a God who does whatever God chooses to do. This is why Job is so incredulous toward the friends' theology. Their God leaves no room for mystery. Their God is predictable, obvious, easily understood. Job has no experience of such a God, nor do Abraham, Hannah, and Eli. This is the God with whom we all must reckon, he says. Anything less than this God is finally no God at all.

We must allow for the experience of Job, the rawness of it, the harshness of it, the pain of it, as we strive to preach the word of this mysterious God. For this is the God who in the mystery of love chose Israel in Egypt and in the mystery of anger rejected those same people through the prophets. This is the God who in the mystery of love saves us in Jesus and in the mystery of anger holds us accountable to that same Jesus. There is no place in our preaching for the God of the friends; such a God finally does not exist at all. Once we are ready to hear that word, we are ready to become Joban preachers.

On Becoming a Joban Preacher

Again and again, Job shouts, howls, and screams for his vindication. In the face of the increasingly angry, resistant, assaultive words of his so-called friends, and in the face of the increasingly frustrating silence of God, Job persists in his demands. And that is one of the genuine wonders of his story. His demands may best be summarized in another look at what must be the most famous lines from the book, 19:23–25 (see the commentary for more extended remarks).

Job is saying nothing here that he has not said previously in his demands for justice. In both 9:33ff. and 16:19–21, he has asked for vindication from some unnamed party, first from an umpire in chapter 9 and then from a witness in chapter 16. Now he announces that there is for him somewhere a vindicator who, either before or after his death—the state of the text will not allow certainty on the matter—will set the crooked record straight. What Job does in this speech is to up the ante a bit. That is, now his case will be chiseled in a rock, the words outlined in molten lead, so that for thousands of years the horror of the injustice done to Job shall be heard and seen by countless generations. He is convinced that, however long it takes, he will be vindicated; his suffering will not have been in vain.

But the real wonder of these words is that Job is still saying them at all. The friends have one final say, and the two of them who do speak a third time reveal the genuine poverty of their beliefs. First Eliphaz astonishingly shouts to Job that God does not at all care whether Job is righteous or not, having little long-term interest in any human being (chap. 22). And Bildad, in a six-verse speech, says to Job that human beings are no better than maggots and worms (25:1–6). Zophar disappears in silence. Thus is the coherent theology of the friends shown to be what Job has said it was almost from the beginning—ashes, clay, thin plaster, a tissue of useless lies.

But Job refuses to give in. In what may be the most glorious speech of all, Job stands up on his ash heap and leaves off scratching his scaly body long enough to hurl amazing words into our astonished ears (27:2–6).

And that is what it means to be a Joban preacher. Do not hear his words only as the ravings of an arrogant man, one who needs a great infusion of humility if he is to come before his God. Job is ready to come before the mysterious God precisely because he refuses to play the theological games of the friends. Job will never admit in any way that they are right. But note, too, that he will never speak injustice or utter deceit. By that he means that he will call a spade a spade, let the chips fall where they may. His raw experience is true for him; he will not disguise it, sweeten it, nuance it, or in any way deny it. Job comes to God as Job, not some approximation of Job, not some Job as he wishes he were, certainly not the Job the friends wanted him to be. The word often used for such a person is integrity.

Integrity is wholeness, completeness, honesty, sincerity. Remarkably enough, Job comes to God unimpaired, though he is penniless, sick, and absolutely alone. Can you see him? Note his tattered and filthy robe, his broken piece of pottery, his sore-ridden body. But now see his face. He is unbowed; he is resolute; he is eager for truth. And God comes to him—not to the friends who know all they need to live the life they want for themselves. God comes to Job, converses with Job, listens to Job, and then says an unforgettable thing that Job only overhears, since it is the *only* thing God says to these friends who thought they knew all. "You have not spoken to me the truth as my servant Job has," says God, and like a house built on sand all of the words of the friends fall to the ground.

And so we must ask what it is Job said that was right about God. The word that God announces about the "rightness" and "truthfulness" of Job's words throughout the dialogue suggest, as Habel has it, that the "blunt and forthright language of Job from the depths of his agony are far closer to the truth of things than those conventional unquestioning pronouncements of the friends."[6] In short, his honest reactions to his raw experience do have value for any who would speak the word of God in any age.

We live in a world surrounded by Jobs, so many who have experienced life in the raw, so many who look at us as Job saw the friends, plasterers of lies, worthless physicians. When we preach, Job must be with us, his painful life must speak to ours, for in him speak the voices of millions of our brothers and sisters in this world. We must become Joban preachers, open to the painful truth of our own lives and the lives of others.

Nothing less will do, for as Job's life has shown, it is to such as these that God chooses to speak God's healing and lifegiving word.

CHAPTER 9

Sermons from Job

Here are two sermons from Job. I have tried to offer sermons of somewhat different kinds in order that they might tease the mind of the reader all the more to active thought, whether about a Joban sermon she/he would like to preach or would like to hear. I have annotated the first sermon with comments in order to describe what I am trying to do as the sermon progresses. This style of sermon presentation has been used often in more recent homiletical books, and I have found it to be very helpful in the evaluation of the sermon.[1] If the reader is distressed by the constant breaking into the flow of the sermon, he/she may skip the comments and read the sermon straight through, returning to the comment sections afterward. Sermon 2 is written right through, with any comments reserved for the end.

An Embodied Sermon

This sermon was preached in the chapel of Perkins School of Theology, Southern Methodist University, on November 6, 1970. I was a seminary student in my final year of study. I was in the third month of a year-long seminar on Job, so I had yet to get to the end of the book or to reflect very much on the meaning of the book as a whole. Hence, this sermon takes as its point of departure a singular idea from one speech. Two thoughts strike me as I read and present this sermon again after nearly thirty years.

First, this sermon was read while my wife, Diana, portrayed the sermon in dance. The beauty and sensitivity of her movements and gestures added immeasurably to the experience of the words. Indeed, she became the living embodiment of what my words were trying to say. Hence, the bare words of the sermon do not begin to convey the physical grace of the experience. I have provided a few vocal directions to suggest how I tried to voice the various parts of the sermon, and I can only ask that you, the reader, attempt to imagine a dancer, dressed in leotard and flowing white skirt, living the words spoken.

Second, the terrible war in Vietnam was raging while this sermon was presented. I am struck, and embarrassed, by the sermon's insularity, its basically parochial concerns about the need for relationships. I do not apologize for my attempt to present this important concern, which is certainly part of the gospel, but I am fully aware that the world context of the sermon was little in evidence. It is obvious to me now, as I peer backward at myself in my third year of seminary, that I had yet to understand the need I had to become a Joban preacher, one who was alert to the pain and anguish of the world, not insulating oneself from the harsh truth that is always with us. I had classmates during that time who were much further along than I on the road to Joban theological maturity, while I had taken but a few tiny steps. Still, here is a sermon from my distant past, and it is a sermon from Job. I hope it provides for you some things to consider about the book and some ideas you may find useful for your own preaching from Job.

"A Friend" (Job 6:14–27)

Picture Job. Perfect and upright. Pious to a fault.
Secure in his riches, his family, and his faith.
A blessed man, a saintly man, favored by God.
Then that God acts.

Job loses his riches, his family, but apparently not his faith.
"Curse God, and die," cries his anguished wife.
Job says, "YHWH gave, YHWH took away.
Blessed be YHWH's name.
Shall we accept good from God, and not accept evil?"

Three friends hear what has happened and come to console and comfort him, this great man brought low. They sit in silence before the loathsome figure they once knew so well, squatting painfully on a little hill made up of the ashes of his life. For seven days and seven nights silence deafens.

But now picture Job. Now his faith, too, is gone.
"Damn the day I was born!
Better to be in Sheol where there is rest.
I have none here.
I yearn for death; I would rejoice to find my grave.
My life is only agony."

What has Job done? He wants death, but YHWH creates life.

Job is a blasphemer. Should we excommunicate him?

What would you say to Job? Let's see what the three friends say.

Listen to them and watch them closely.

Comment

I have tried in these very brief lines to sketch the substance of the prologue. I telescoped the assaults on Job into one response, calling what happened an act of God, but not raising the issue of the test between God and the Satan. In my teaching of the book, I have discovered that too much time is often spent worrying about this scene, to the detriment of the much more important drama to follow. As my commentary attempted to show, the YHWH/the Satan scene is merely one used by the poet to raise the theological and anthropological questions that are paramount: What sort of God is it who has created the universe, and what is the appropriate stance of a human being in relation to that God?

In five lines I tried to summarize chapter 3's monologue, focusing on Job's rejection of God's good gift of life in order that the listener could hear it for the blasphemy it would be in the ears of ancient Israelites. With the question, "What would you say to Job?" I raise the issue of the sermon. I want to confront the hearers with the very unpleasant ideas that the supposedly faithful Job begins to utter, and challenge them to listen to what he has to say without "turning him off" too quickly. Job wants to be heard; can we hear the Jobs among us?

Please remember that the dance is going on as I speak. I have attempted to read the words with as much drama as I can muster, raising my voice in the frustration of Job's wife, offering Job's calm response first, but then adding a dash of uncertainty when he asks his question as a second response. The summary of chapter 3 is full of scorn and bitterness; I strain my voice in fury and rage. When the third-person speaker reappears, after a pause I lower my voice conversationally. At the end of that comment, before the friends begin to come, I pause at length to prepare the listener for their coming.

Eliphaz the friend speaks first. He is a man who knows, has seen, and can demonstrate the truth about God. He is a holy man, blessed with visitations of the supernatural. "Is not your hope your perfect conduct? All of those who sow evil reap the same. No innocent one has ever been destroyed. And I'll prove to you the truth I speak. One night, in a trance just like Abraham's, Ezekiel's, and Jeremiah's, I heard a strange voice, felt strange wisps of air across my face. My hair stood right on end! And the voice said, 'Can a mortal be just before God?' You fool, Job! Recant, admit your guilt. If only you had the understanding we three have, you would also know the truth."

Does Eliphaz look familiar? Oh, perhaps few of us would claim the authority of visions, but how very easy it is to say, "Well, since I read Hebrew and Greek, I'll reveal to you what the Bible really says." Or, "I tithe; I teach; God surely must love me—sorry about you." We are not so foreign to Eliphaz. We too forget that we are only people after all, subject to the same shortcomings and lack of knowledge as is everyone else. Job needs a friend. What would you say to Job? How would you respond?

Comment

I have attempted to create the character of Eliphaz as I have described him in the commentary. He is a man of substance, supremely confident, beautifully well spoken. Hence, I round my tone and lower the pitch enough to give him weight and stature. And I slow my pace appreciably. Eliphaz is never in a hurry; he knows the truth and knows exactly how to say it for maximum effect.

The points are two: Innocence is always rewarded just as certainly as wickedness is always punished by a God of the strictest justice; and Eliphaz has been visited from on high, that is, he has a direct line to God. Thus, his beliefs can brook no argument since their origin is divine. Eliphaz presents the worst sort of arrogance, the sort that is based on unchallengeable grounds. When he speaks, he never expects any disagreement, only awed and thorough approval and acceptance, followed by complete repentance to the position espoused by Eliphaz. He has not so much answered Job; he has summarily and haughtily repudiated his right to speak at all. That, of course, is all the answer that a blasphemer like Job deserves.

But, much to Eliphaz' surprise and shock, Job not only speaks, but retorts with real heat.

And now Job speaks. "I have a right to scream. God has struck me down. You speak of hope. Am I as strong as stones? Do I have any help from within me? All is gone; I have no hope!

"Hope is only a thread, and I want that thread cut. My hope is at the end of the thread of life.

"Teach me, and I will listen. Help me!

"But *you*! You are like a river that dries up in the heat of the day! Like a desert mirage that vanishes when a caravan hopes for shade. A sick person should have the loyalty of a friend. Even if he renounces God! God, leave me alone! But, help me…someone!"

Isn't Job insufferable! We see that he had a good life, but he has completely forgotten that and goes on and on that his whole life has been pain from beginning to end. Why, how ungrateful can a person be! He should count his blessings! Why, all sorts of folk are a lot worse off than he! Besides, where there is smoke, there is fire! Not just anyone ends up on a pile of ashes. He could get work, you know!

Do you feel like saying any of those things? When you see and hear Job, does revulsion well up inside you? Perhaps. But Job still needs a friend. What would you say?

Comment

I do a very quick summary of chapters 5 and 6, focusing on 6:14 and following. Job's speech now is riddled with scorn and sarcasm. He snaps out the vowels and bites off the consonants. But like much scorn and sarcasm, there is also desperation, a grasping at whatever straws might be floating by in the wind. Job very early sees that these friends are not going to hear him and, thus, they are not going to be able to answer him. All this must be done in short strokes. Of course, my words were much aided by the dance that filled the eye and the heart in ways that the words alone could never quite do.

I step out of the drama to comment, making sure that the listener remains confronted both by the inadequacies of Job's friends, the darkly bitter ways in which Job attacks them, and the need for the listeners to find some appropriate ways to respond to this loudmouth of the ash heap.

Bildad the friend speaks. His answers are quick and sure, for he is a church historian. He knows the traditions of the faith. "Just ask former generations; consider the lore of the ancestors. Does God pervert justice? Our traditions say no! Job, you simply cannot be right, for the hope of the impious will perish. You said you wanted to perish, didn't you? Well, what is one to conclude from that? You need to repent. Yes, you need to repent, as our traditions tell us, and then you will be saved!"

"Yes, these are hard times, my friends," we hear ourselves saying. "But remember the great faith of Moses, Amos, Jesus. Read your Bible! God said it, I believe it, and that's the end of it." All of us know Bildad only too well. Job needs a friend, not now the wise sayings of Martin Luther, not now the strength of ecclesiastical authority, not now even a well-chosen quote from the scriptures. Obnoxious as Job is, he needs a friend. What would you say to Job?

Comment

Again, we find our portrayal of Bildad from the commentary. He is an academic, as certain as Eliphaz, but very different in tone and manner. He is quick, high-strung, a bit disheveled, in the business of expounding the meaning of things to those who are eager for his enlightenment. I pitch my voice much higher than for Eliphaz, and I move my speech right along, focusing on Bildad's beliefs that Job has revealed his sin out of his own mouth, and that the witness of the ancestors is that Job is in desperate need of repentance.

Because this sermon was first given in a seminary chapel, the portrait of Bildad had, and has, special resonance. However, any church has its Bildads, both in pulpit and in pew. Any time one decides to end a discussion with a judicious quote from the riches of the theological past, spreading erudition rather than love among the unwashed mass, "pearls before swine" as one ancient prophet had it, Bildad is alive and well.

But the issue remains for the listener: How are we to hear Job and be for him a friend? How are the Jobs of our lives to be included in our communities? What are our responsibilities for and to them?

Job responds. "I know all that; that God is magnificent, moves mountains, shakes the earth, commands the sun, stretches out the heavens. But how can one be righteous before God? I would like to reason with God about this, but though I am righteous, God would condemn me. Though guiltless, God would say I am perverse. But I am innocent! Put aside your wrath and power for a while, and let's talk.

"Oh, what's the use! Innocent or guilty, it's all the same. Get away, God! Let me smile just once before I gurgle my last breath and croak!"

Doesn't Job make you uncomfortable? Doesn't he make you sick? Don't you just want to wring his neck? Don't you just want him to get off it? Why not say: "Now we see in a mirror dimly, but then face to face"? Or, "When we all get to heaven, oh how happy we will be." Or, "Woe to you who strive with your maker like a clay pot with the potter!"

Sounds like Eliphaz or Bildad to me! But he still needs a friend, though "friends" are all around. Just what would you do?

Comment

Job knows what the tradition has told him about the power of God, and what the friends continue to preach about the retributive justice of the universe, but these traditional beliefs are flying in the face of a life of struggle, frustration, and agony. Can no one listen long enough to the obnoxious Job really to hear what he is trying to say?

Again, I try to make modern-day application of ideas people have long used to speak to sufferers, words uttered with the best of intentions that often have had the most painful effects. "God wanted her more than you." "We just have to trust God, since God always has the right plan." "Time heals all wounds." Much truth may be locked up in these phrases, but in the presence of intense suffering, they often strike like hammer blows on the heads and like electric shocks in the hearts of the sufferers. Hence, I wanted to raise up the ways that we, in the face of our Jobs, do indeed sound like Eliphaz and Bildad.

But Job is still after a friend. How can we be one for him?

Zophar the friend speaks. He speaks for God, because he knows exactly how God acts. He knows God's great power, God's infinite strength. Little Job can hardly plumb the depths of God. "Puny beings like you will get wisdom on the same day that a wild donkey gives birth to a human child. In other words, never! Stretch out your hand to God. Then will your face be cleansed. The wicked have no hope, which is what you said, Job! How right you are, you sniveling, weaseling, lying, blaspheming, disgusting little twerp!"

Ah, Zophar said what we would like to say: "Job, you are really too much! Come on, join the human race. Get off your high horse, admit that you are hardly what you claim to be, and come back to the truth. You are the only one who thinks all of us are wrong. What does that tell you, huh? You can hardly be the only one right in the entire universe!"

Comment

I have tried to capture the cruel bluntness of Zophar, who has little time for polite dialogue. He tells Job that God has all the wisdom and all the power, and unless Job 'fesses up and turns abjectly to God, his doom is assured. Again, my portrait of Zophar in the commentary determines his portrayal in the sermon. He is a modern man "on the make," beautifully dressed with the right shoes, the right shirt, the right tie. The correct model may be a Hollywood movie producer, "shmoozing" with money and prestige and power.

His voice should be unctuous, oily. His manner nonchalant, yet persistent. He is all right, and Job is all wrong. There is only one way to think and act, and it is not Job's way. Job's consistent rejection of Zophar and his two companions has made Zophar's blood boil, but he does not want to "lose his cool," so he merely states what he knows beyond doubt to be true about God and about Job. The emphasis should fall on the words "know" and "no hope." Zophar "knows," and Job has "no hope."

But Job has one more speech to make to these three would-be counselors and friends.

"I repeat. I know all that, but the facts are: I am innocent, and my hope is gone.

"But what about you, you quacks? Can you trick God as you trick people? Your sayings, your wisdom, your learning, your visions are ashen to me and to God. Just listen to me for a change. Shut your mouths long enough to listen! Are you my friends, or not? Why treat me as God does, like some sort of enemy? I am trapped and alone on the hill of no hope, God-less and friendless. I am innocent before God. All God can do is kill me—I'd even like that, I guess.

"But what of you? I live with and among you. Let's talk; you listen to me, then I'll listen to you. You said, Zophar, to reach out. I am reaching out—to you, and to you, and to you. In a world of lonely ash heaps, I need a friend."

Comment

The sermon idea was generated from my translation of 6:14: "As for those who deny kindness to a friend: they abandon the worship of Shaddai!" True friendship, says Job, ought not be based on similar beliefs, on certain prescribed modes of behavior, on acceptable styles of speaking. Friendship should be given freely, even to one who appears to have forsaken all traditional beliefs and practices. Friendship should be as God should be, devoted and loyal and loving no matter what. That is why Job uses the word "kindness" (chesed) to characterize true friendship. As I noted in the commentary, it is this Hebrew word that, in the tradition, best describes the basic way of God with the world.

Job presents to all of us the extreme test of our willingness to reach out to those who are radically unlike us. If I were to preach this sermon again, I would want to focus much more specifically on current experiences of my own inability and/or unwillingness to include such persons or groups into my circle of friendship and caring. In my attempts to become a more mature Joban preacher I have learned to name openly my own shortcomings in order that I can receive the forgiveness from God I need to move forward to a more inclusive life, to a community that more closely resembles the realm of God.

I feel the sermon, in very brief but very focused ways, suggested how we were still living manifestations of the three friends. It needs more work in delineating just who Job is for us modern Eliphazes, Bildads, and Zophars. He is the outsider, the marginalized, the radical unbeliever, the challenger of my comfort, the upsetter of my cart. I need to hear him, but I find that task nearly impossible for me. He cries out to me still.

I would name this sermon type a reflective narrative, and I would add it to the five types of narrative sermons I delineated in an earlier work on narrative preaching.[2] A part of Job's story forms the backbone of the sermon, but after each narrative section I break in to comment on what I am trying to do in the narrative. In my understanding of narrative sermons, I tend to use narrative material in this way quite rarely, because I am convinced that the Bible's stories need to be heard and told with as little comment as possible in order that they can be received again into our post-biblical church communities. Still, a reflective narrative such as this one could be a helpful way both to offer the story to the hearer and to make immediately apparent what possible meanings the story may have for the contemporary listener.

A Narrative Sermon

I wish now to present a sermon in what I have called a pure narrative style.[3] I will tell the story of Job in such a way as to allow the hearer to hear the whole thing, or at least to hear one possible way to hear the whole thing. This style assumes intimate acquaintance with the work of the commentary, because I must pick and choose from the vast possibilities presented by the plot in order to get the story into a hearable frame, both in terms of length and in terms of meaning. Of course, no one tells a story without loading that story with the meaning the teller has in mind. I hope at many points in the sermon to signal that meaning to the listener so that the story can become sermon, a presentation of the good news of God.

This sermon was preached at St. Paul's United Methodist Church in Muskogee, Oklahoma, on February 9, 1997, during the course of a series of sermons in that congregation.

"Truth to God" Job 42:1–6

Believe me, I am as surprised as you! To be back in the community, surrounded by friends and family, playing with my great-great grandchildren, enjoying three beautiful daughters and seven robust sons. You should have asked me just a short while ago what I thought my chances were of seeing all this! This, all this, is nothing less than an astonishing gift from the bounty of God. Yes, a gift of God; I can say that now. For most of my life, I did not know what the word "gift" meant. When I remember the way I used to be! When I remember what happened...

Long ago I was rich, comfortable, big house, fine clothes, servants at my call, lovely wife, ten wonderful children, respected by everyone. But, my comfort was really only skin-deep. Inside, I was scared. I just knew that what I had I could lose any time. I used to lie awake nights, picturing my things in my head. Each sheep, each donkey, each camel, every field, each bulging bank account, over and over they would turn, as I thrashed around in my monarch-sized bed. I knew I had not done enough. Oh, I went to church—my, my, did I go to church! I spent hours and hours and hours in church.

I knew my ten kids were fine; they were all good kids, the best any father could want. But I kept wondering, especially about these parties they always had. Every time there would be a birthday or an anniversary of some kind or a new job or a good grade, one of them would throw a party. And that one would, without fail, invite his or her nine siblings to join in the fun. Well, you know kids nowadays! What with drugs and booze and sex and wild music and wild dancing—there was no telling what sorts of unspeakable mischief one or more of them could get involved with. So, me? I went to church after every party, every party! I didn't miss a one!

And every time I went, I dragged along ten animals for sacrifice, one for each of them. Talk about expensive! My sacrifices at one time accounted for nearly 45 percent of my total income! But what else could I do? You see, I just knew that God, the Almighty Creator of us all, was ready to pounce on whatever sin one of my kids may have committed. What was true for me was just as true for them. That is why I have always been so careful to do nothing that possessed even the hint of wrongdoing, the slightest whiff of sin. After all, I was absolutely certain that God rewarded those who kept their noses clean and punished those who messed up or messed around.

That is what I had always been taught at church, and I had learned those church lessons well. This God was nobody to be trifled with, and I had no intention of trifling. So I sacrificed and sacrificed and sacrificed until I could hardly get the smell of roasted oxen out of my clothes or out of my nose. But at least I knew I was safe. God would surely do nothing to someone who was so holy, so saintly, so pious; so I had been taught.

And so I thought. My, my, was I wrong! One terrible day, my whole life unraveled. These four strangers came to me and announced that my livestock and some of my servants had been killed by a marauding band of Sabeans, and some more livestock and servants had died in a freakish storm, and my prize camels and the rest of the servants had been slaughtered by some Chaldeans, and finally that my children—all ten!—had died during one of those parties, those wretched parties. The house had collapsed on all of them.

What could I say? What would you say? I blessed the God who can take as well as give. I once had nothing and became rich and now had nothing again. That's what I said. But what I thought was, "It's happened! I knew it! One of those kids, or even I, must have crossed the line, and God had to act in the way God always acts." I remained pious in the only way I knew how. I took it; it was God. What could I say?

But then I got this repulsive disease, and I don't mean the heartbreak of psoriasis! I cannot bear to describe it—running sores, tightening scabs, breaking out again, more running sores. And the itching, such itching. It was nothing less than the sixth plague of Egypt! I grabbed all that was left of the rubble of my beautiful kitchen, a broken piece of our finest crockery, and started to scrape those sores. I went to sleep night after night still scraping, scraping. My lovely wife urged me to pack it in. Bless her, she was so worried about me, about her ruined life, about our dead children, I could not blame her. She said to go ahead and curse God so that God would be forced to end my misery. Well, I couldn't do it, not yet. I mean, this was God we were talking about! Curse God? Still, she did have a point. And when I spoke in response, what came from my mouth was not a confident statement, but a question laced with wondering. "Shall we accept good from God and not accept evil?" Well, should we?

Then *they* showed up. Yes, they, Eliphaz, Bildad, and Zophar. I could tell right off that they had already made up their minds about me before they had even opened their mouths. They stood a long way off and tossed dust up in the air on their own heads, hoping to avoid what had come upon me. They knew, they thought, what had happened. They saw me on my hill of ashes, covered with suppurating sores, abandoned, and alone. They just knew that I had done *something*. Something unspeakable, something disgusting, to have received all of this from the God who could be counted on always to reward and punish in the clearest of ways. I knew they knew, and I imagine they knew that I knew they knew. Anyway, there was a very long silence.

Well, I looked at them, and I looked at the ruin that used to be my house, and I gave my sores a good long scrape, and I knew I had had enough. Enough of the old verities. Enough of the old expectations. Enough of the old simple pieties. My life was a shambles, and I had had enough.

And so I cursed. I cursed the day of my birth. I cursed the night of my conception. I cursed the light and the dark. Out of my mouth came the most creative curses, some even I had never heard from my less religious buddies. And I came close to cursing God even then, wondering out loud what God was doing, making a hellhole like this life and then hiding its meaning from everyone in it. I just had to say it, get it off my chest. It was like a great primal scream. I really didn't intend for it to be taken as some sort of serious opinion, some reasoned argument about the structure of the universe. It was just a big, loud exhalation of painful breath.

But wouldn't you know it, those three took it all very seriously! They heard in what I said all sorts of things I didn't say and certainly didn't mean. But I soon learned that they really weren't listening to me; they just had a whole bunch of things they were dying to say, so they thought they would use my pain as the forum for saying it. When they first started up, I thought it was all a kind of joke. But I noticed quickly that none of them were laughing.

"Isn't your piety your confidence, your integrity your hope?" intoned that windbag Eliphaz. "Nobody who was really innocent ever got bad stuff from the universe." Well, it didn't take a Ph.D. to figure out what the old boy meant. He meant me. I had gotten bad stuff from the universe—that was about as obvious as it gets!—and so I simply could not be innocent. *Oh, yeah?* I thought. Eliphaz really got my goat, and I could not let him get away without a few choice comments. So I told him I was screaming so loudly because God was using me for target practice, and God's poisoned arrows were a real pain. And I also said that if he were any kind of friend at all, he would show some pity to me, rather than being so intent on classing me with the foul sinners of the world. I mean, I've known some foul sinners in my time, and I sure was not one of them. Anyone who knew me knew that. Then I said in as many ways as I could that I wished I were dead. And I did, believe me.

Now, you have to remember that all four of us believed roughly the same things about God. We all thought God did it all, and we all thought that God *did* reward and punish. But after my experiences, I began to wonder about that. I even accused God of confusing me with the great monster of the sea, Yam. Maybe that's why God thought I needed to be attacked and controlled. Maybe God had had a hard day. Or maybe God was just losing it; running a universe, I assume, can be exhausting work, could take the zip out of a person. Maybe God needed a sabbatical. Whatever I said, I certainly did not do what that old spooky Eliphaz expected. If he thought I would quietly say, "Gosh, I never thought of that, you wise man," he was badly disappointed.

His running buddy, Bildad, put his oar in too. He had the gall to say directly that God killed my kids because they deserved it! Can you believe that? After that line popped out of his erudite little mouth, I didn't listen all that carefully to the rest of his disgusting speech. But I let him have it when he was done. I told him I had heard all that crazy stuff before, and I was having a very hard time believing it anymore, given the mess my life had become. I said God was powerful, but not gracious, as far as I could see. In fact, I went a step further. I said that God killed everyone, righteous and wicked, and laughed when they all died! Oh, you should have seen their faces when I said that! But what else could I believe? Something was terribly wrong in the universe, and since God was the main actor, there had to be something wrong with God, as far as I was able to see.

Then I said that I wished there were some kind of umpire around to make it possible for me to talk to God without being afraid. But I knew deep down that if I ever got the chance, God would just show off that power, storm around asking a slew of questions I could never answer, and pay about as much attention to me as those friends of mine did. So I talked some more about wishing to die and imagined that that was the end of this little discussion. Boy, was I wrong again!

Then Zophar, wise guy, said—get this—that a stupid person (my, I wonder who he means?) will get smart on the same day that a donkey gives birth to a human! Well, I have to admit, that was a good one! But since it was directed at me, I had to say something to shut that twit up. What I said was, "No doubt when you die all wisdom will die with you!" Not bad, not bad. Not quite as good as donkeys giving birth to humans, but not bad! These jerks were not helpful, and any thought that they were in any way my friends was completely wrong.

I wish I could tell you that things picked up between us, but they didn't. Far from it! They got madder and madder, and I got madder and madder. They drove me to it; they just could not leave well enough alone. The more they ranted and raved about my sin and God's punishment, the more I was convinced that they were wrong. They convinced me, yes, those three fools, that I did not deserve what I was getting. I finally decided that I did not wish to die at all. What I wanted was to meet God. I wanted to have it out with God! I knew that I was right, and God was wrong. If I could just find God—in the street, in a house, in a courtroom, someplace. I wanted vindication in the eyes of the world and, most of all, in the eyes of God.

I even went so far—you may not believe this as you look at me now, surrounded by God's own gifts—to imagine that there was some sort of heavenly attorney who was going to take my case and win it against God! But that wasn't the half of it. I even imagined that there was a powerful avenger who, upon understanding the injustice that had been done to me, would seek God out in order to kill God, thus righting the imbalance of the world brought on by God's monstrous actions. I tell you,

I was desperate! My view of God forced me to want what I deserved. I had been good, and I wanted those wonderful material things reserved for the good.

You can imagine how horrified those friends were by that kind of talk! So they blustered on, trying to get me to buy their lunacy about my evil and God's justice, but my experience told me different. Finally, they shut up, thank God, but not before Eliphaz admitted, in his own confused way, that God didn't really care whether anyone was righteous or wicked (what I had said several times myself), and not before Bildad blubbered that he thought human beings were worms and maggots. Now there was a helpful and uplifting thought! Thank heaven, that fool Zophar had nothing more to say at all. I guess that good donkey line was the best he had.

I proceeded to talk only to God. I told God that I had done nothing to deserve what I had gotten, and just to make the point, I went through an elaborate oath of innocence, daring God, really forcing God, to prove it otherwise. I expected God to come. Now it was my turn to be surprised, because this snot-nosed kid named Elihu appeared. He was hilarious at first. It took him forever to get to the point of talking, even though he talked a long time about it! He had me laughing, I'll tell you, but then he got to the same stuff those other three had gone on about, and I stopped laughing. But, my, he could talk! About halfway through I admit I stopped listening, so I can't begin to tell you what he said. However, toward the end, I did hear him say that God was never in a million years going to show up to talk to me. By that time, after his gazillion words, I thought he might be right about that, but then we both got a surprise. God showed up. That's right. God, YHWH, came and started to speak to me, to Job, old loud-mouthed Job.

But, you know what? By that time I could not begin to hear what God was saying to me. Oh, I half-listened to a lot of stuff about seas and ice and snow and wind. And then there was a bunch of talk about ravens and lions and ostriches—ostriches for goodness' sake! It sounded to me exactly like I thought it would, sound and fury, signifying nothing, with no attention at all to my concerns about justice and vindication. Frankly, I was miffed! And so in the face of that bluster, I shut up. That's all, I just shut up.

But that was hardly the end, and am I ever glad! God refused to take my silence for an answer. God tried a different tack in another speech. First, I learned that God had been listening to me after all. I knew that when God said, "Would you make me wrong so that you can be in the right?" Well, I thought, yes! I would! That is the point, and I half-imagined that God might begin an apology of some sort to me, the wronged party. But it turned out I was the wrong party, because then I heard God tell me to treat the wicked like I thought they were treated, you know, swatted down, flattened. "Go on, Job," God said, "let's see some real wicked bashing!" I noticed that when God said it there was a hint of amusement in the divine voice and a bemused twinkle in the divine eye. God knew I couldn't do it, and I thought God was just making fun of me again. I should have guessed right then that I couldn't do it, because God didn't act like that either. The best surprise was still to come.

Suddenly, God opened the divine throne room a crack and out rumbled two great creatures I had only dreamt of in my wildest nightmares. They were Behemoth and Leviathan, monsters of land and sea. What were they doing in God's place? What had they to do with God? And then God said, "I made these, Job, just as I made you." All at once, the images of that first speech came back to me, and I began to see it. The world of God was not at all what I and my friends had thought, not even close. It was a place of mystery. Rain fell on uninhabitable lands; ravens were fed the blood of other creatures who died so that they might live; ostriches, silly and deprived of any sense, left their eggs on the ground to be crushed by any passing thing, but God made them and sustained them, too. And if that weren't enough, terrible Behemoth and nasty Leviathan were also in the world and important parts of it. The world was not the mechanical, easily understood, readily appropriated place I had been taught it was.

And because the world was like that, neither was God like I thought God was. The God I now saw struggled with the wonders of the world God made and did not establish it to operate at the beck and call of any human behaviors. Yes, what God showed me was a world dangerous and wondrous, often quite unpredictable, often quite lovely, even quite hilarious. In short, what God showed me was that freedom and grace were alive in the world and God was the author of both.

So, now you can understand why I spoke as I did at the end. I marveled at my new vision of God. I wondered at the fact that I was not condemned by God, and I learned that neither did I have to condemn God to find a rightful place in the cosmos. I retracted all my blather about God. I did not repent of the way I spoke, the passion with which my furious words were uttered. I had been granted a new view of God, so new that I am still trying to catch all that it might mean for me.

And so now here I am playing with my great-great grandchildren. They, and everything you see around me, are gifts of God. No, God did not reward me with these things. How ridiculous that would have been! The whole point is that no human behavior determines how God reacts in God's world. Yes, I prayed for my friends; yes, they offered up some sacrifices for themselves. But these acts were performed not for gain, but because God asked us to do them.

How easy it is to assume that somehow my actions, whether good or bad, demand the reactions of God. How easy it is to assume that I am in the very center of God's creation, and that all things revolve around me, around my needs. How easy to forget the mystery and wonder and surprise that the cosmos holds every day. How easy to confine God into some sort of formula, some kind of equation. Believe me, friends, I have a new way of seeing, and though I cannot understand it all, and neither can you, we both can live together in a community of those who accept our rightful places in God's world. We can live our lives knowing that freedom is the hallmark of God and grace the hallmark of God's gifts to us. So, come. Join us in the community of prayer and feasting, created and sustained by the God of mystery and wonder, the God of freedom and of grace. Come on! I've saved some food just for you.

Comment

This is what I have called a pure narrative sermon. I have told the story, using Job himself as my teller, having him flash back through his experience. *Using Job like this has at least two advantages. First, he provides an immediacy to the story because it is his. He has lived through it and can share it with us accordingly. And, of course, it is his journey toward newness that we trace in the tale. Second, by flashing back as he does, he becomes both first-person teller and third-person observer. That is, he can both recount his experience and can comment on its meaning at the same time. He is thus a perfect interlocutor for this kind of sermon.*[4]

I did not this time provide a running commentary, because I think you can see quite easily which portions of the text I have chosen for this telling to attempt to address the question of Job's new understanding of God as opposed to his former understanding. You need only review the commentary to discover those places.

Perhaps a few words should be said about why I made the choices I did. The goal of a pure narrative sermon must be kept clear throughout the telling. Hence, however much I might be attracted to the rich portrayal of the friends, in a telling of the whole story, I cannot dwell on them. Because I believe that the keys to this reading are found in the speeches of God and the responses of Job, I must tell enough of how we arrive at that place to provide suitable plot context, but not so much that no one cares by the time we arrive! In short, I try to do orally what the text does verbally. That is, I cannot spend the time orally that the words spend visually, because the ear will tire sooner than the eye. I must keep the plot moving if I hope to keep my listeners with me as we thread our way through this complex plot.

I would hope that any preachers reading this book would ask themselves at this point which parts of the book they would choose to tell the entire story of Job. And I hope that any listeners to sermons would ask themselves which parts they need to hear in order to grasp the sense of the whole. A conversation between these two groups could prove very fruitful for both.

The poem of Job announces in brilliant art what the Hebrews said again and again about their God: that God is free to act and is in bondage to no one or nothing. But more. Our proper stance in the face of this radically free God of wonder and surprise is the unending search for truth in a world of real pain and real hardship and real struggle. We cannot confine ourselves to the old ways alone, no matter how sweet and pleasant their songs. There are real Jobs in the world, persons who are suffering in innocence, persons who are forgotten by the world. As long as these Jobs cry out for justice, no preacher may close his/her ears to those cries and hope to preach the good news of God. Like latter-day Jacobs, we preachers and listeners find ourselves wrestling with what we think to be God, but upon awakening, really awakening, we find that God for us is not our opponent but rather our fellow struggler, striving with us toward the truth of things, searching with us for the shalom of the world, a world that always includes our Jobs. Indeed, it was not until Jacob saw his brother, Esau, poor, old, foolish, and pathetic Esau, that he could say, "Seeing your face is like seeing the face of God" (Gen. 33:10). May all of us see the face of God in the Jobs of the world. And may all of us, including our Jobs, see God for who God is, Creator and Sustainer of a wondrous world, the friend all of us need to create a community of justice wherein all find their place.

NOTES

Preface

[1]H. Kallen in *The Book of Job as a Greek Tragedy Restored* (New York: Moffat, Yard & Co., 1918), attempted to demonstrate how the poem shared many affinities to a supposed Greek tragic style. Samuel Terrien in a 1969 article made some very tentative suggestions concerning the use of the poem as a "para-ritual drama" designed for performance during the Israelite celebration of the New Year; see "Le Poem de Job: drame para-rituel du nouvel-an?" *Vetus Testamentum Supplement* 17 (1969): 220–35. See David J. A. Clines, *Job 1–20*, Word Biblical Commentary, vol. 17 (Dallas: Word Books, 1989), cxiv–cxv, for further references to commentators who have found the dramatic analogy fruitful, with the Greek connection the most popular.

Chapter 1: The Prologue (Job 1—2)

[1]In the prologue the word translated "curse" in 1:5, 11; 2:5, 9 is actually in the Hebrew text the word *baraq*, "bless." Early readers of the story may have changed the text from an original *killelu*, "curse," in order to keep the word of cursing far away from the name of God. Pope calls it a "standard scribal emendation"; Marvin Pope, *Job* (Garden City, N.Y.: Doubleday, 1973), 8; see also Hartley, *The Book of Job* (Grand Rapids: Eerdmans, 1988), 65.

[2]Archibald MacLeish, *JB*, (Boston: Houghton Mifflin, 1956), 50.

[3]John C. Holbert, *Preaching Old Testament* (Nashville: Abingdon Press, 1991), 87–88.

[4]David J. A. Clines, *Job 1–20*, Word Biblical Commentary, vol. 17 (Dallas: Word Books, 1989), 43–45.

Chapter 2: Job 3

[1]Many modern commentators state that the author of chapter 3 is in fact a different author than the one who wrote the prologue. But most go on to say that the author of 3 adapted the earlier-written prologue for particular purposes. For a detailed consideration of the question, see Samuel L. Terrien, *The Book of Job*, The Interpreter's Bible 3 (Nashville: Abingdon Press, 1954), 884–88, and G. Fohrer, "Zur Vorgeschichte und Komposition des Buches Hiob," *VT* 6 (1956): 249–67.

[2]At the beginning of creation, God had called forth light from the watery darkness of *tohu wabohu* ("formless void," NRSV). God immediately separated the light into "day" and "night," the latter appearing when the former disappeared. Job launches his angry demands by calling for the death of one specific day and one specific night. What God has first created Job would now like to see destroyed.

[3]Leviathan is the violent monster of the sea who is subdued by God in primeval times (see Ps. 74:14; Isa. 27:1). God's defeat of the monster has confined it to the watery deeps wherein, as Ps. 104:26 has it, the creature

187

now "plays." It appears that God has reduced the once-fearsome creature to God's own rubber ducky! But Job clearly has no child's toy in mind.

⁴The nature of the ensuing dialogue has been long discussed. There has been much argument to the effect that the dialogue between Job and his friends is in fact no dialogue at all. The language of the texts suggests otherwise. The Job–friends dialogue employs a technique that could be called "being hoist on one's own petard." This old expression describes a kind of conversation wherein the parties to the discussion listen very carefully to their conversation partners and then use the specific words and phrases of that partner in their own speeches in order to score points against the partner's position. Such a technique is familiar to all.

In a recent campaign for the presidency of the United States, day after day, the rival candidates attempted to hoist one another on their own petards. In one candidate's mouth, the word "liberal" means progressive, forward-thinking, moving with energy and commitment toward a better future. To the other candidate, his opponent's claim to be liberal precisely damns him as the big-government, free-spending, loose-living liar that the word liberal so obviously implies to him and his most ardent supporters. Thus, liberal may be pronounced the same by both candidates, but the second one attempts to "hoist" his opponent by using the word against him, though the meaning of the word to the two of them could not be more different. The discussion is certainly genuine dialogue.

Chapter 3: The First Cycle (Job 4—14)

¹See, for example, Clines, *Job 1–20*, 121; Terrien, *The Book of Job*, 932–36, although Terrien does see the possibilities of irony in his further discussion of Eliphaz' speech, 937–38.

²See, for example, H. H. Rowley, *Job*, The Century Bible (London: Thomas Nelson & Sons, 1970), 50. Rowley quotes A. B. Davidson's 1918 commentary as saying that Eliphaz' first speech is marked by "great delicacy and consideration" and is "very wise and considerate as well as profoundly reverential." Yet even Davidson, he notes, found the speech to be a failure due to the fact that it was "too cold, and too little tempered with compassion for the sufferings of men [sic]." Rowley agrees, saying that Eliphaz' theology "has dried the springs of true sympathy."

³See Rowley, *Job*, 71–72, for a defense of this reading. The text as it stands is scarcely readable; my reading (see NRSV) assumes that Job utters the line as an accusation against the cruelties of Eliphaz, who has clearly "withheld kindness from a friend."

⁴MacLeish, *JB*, 14.

⁵I translate v. 5: "Derision for calamity!" as the thought of the comfortable: "Attack the one who stumbles along!"

⁶Clines, *Job 1–20*, 307–10.

⁷It is well known that the ancient Hebrews had no notion of eternal life resembling the ones developed very late in their own tradition and in the traditions of Christianity and Islam. A balanced introductory discussion of the history of the idea of eternal life may be found in the article "Life" by O. A. Piper in *The Interpreter's Dictionary of the Bible*, vol. 3 (Nashville: Abingdon Press, 1962), 124–31; see also the helpful discussion of the impact of this lack of such a belief in Israel in Walther Eichrodt, *Theology of the Old Testament* (Philadelphia: Westminster, 1961), 424–33.

Chapter 4: The Second Cycle (Job 15—21)

[1]The caricature of Deuteronomy's claims about the ways one can supposedly insure that things "may go well with you" are very old; the book of Job's assault on the notion is proof enough of that. However, that it is a caricature is clear when it is noted that the heart of Deuteronomy's claims is found in chapter 7:7–8. The first action of the covenant is always YHWH's; hence any claim that our actions determine YHWH's actions is plainly false. For further discussion of this notion, see Ronald J. Allen and John C. Holbert, *Holy Root, Holy Branches* (Nashville: Abingdon Press, 1995), 38–42.

[2]H. Haag, "*chamas*," *Theological Dictionary of the Old Testament*, vol. 4, ed. G. Johannes Botterweck and Helmer Ringgren, trans. David E. Green (Grand Rapids: Eerdmans, 1980), 479.

[3]The literature is vast. In addition to the major commentaries, I point the reader to Robert Gordis, *The Book of God and Man* (Chicago: University of Chicago Press, 1965) for a discussion of the verses (pp. 85–91), essentially duplicated in his commentary of 1978 (pp. 178–80). Gordis, along with a host of commentators, assumes that Job's witness of 16:19 is God.

[4]Once again, the literature is vast. Along with the discussions of the commentaries, several special analyses should be noted: J. Speer, "Zur Exegese von Hiob 19:25–27," *ZAW* 25 (1905): 47–140, offers an excellent summary of the pre-twentieth–century commentary on the verses; Theophile Meek, "Job 19:25–27," *VT* 6 (1956): 100–103, tries to show that no textual emendations are needed to gain a clear sense of the lines–no one has followed him in this; J. K. Zink, "Impatient Job: An Interpretation of Job 19:25–27," *JBL* 84 (1965): 147–52 offers a cogent analysis.

[5]See Fohrer, *Das Buch Hiob*, 317; Hartley, *The Book of Job*, 291; Clines, *Job 1–20*, 456–57. Other commentators, following Pope, *Job*, 143, refer to the famous copper scrolls of Qumran as an example closer to hand of what the poet may have had in mind. However, even Pope finds the Behistun inscription of Darius to be a possible model (144).

[6]See the extended discussion of the meanings of this word by Helmer Ringgren in *Theological Dictionary of the Old Testament*, 2, "*ga'al/go'el*," 350–55.

[7]See Alyce M. McKenzie, *Preaching Proverbs* (Louisville: Westminster John Knox Press, 1996), 48–50 for a helpful discussion of the word; and Leo G. Perdue, *Wisdom and Creation* (Nashville: Abingdon Press, 1994), 206–8.

Chapter 6: Job 28—37

[1]Habel, *The Book of Job* (1985), 391–95.

[2]See the classic discussion of the form of the lament in Hermann Gunkel and Joachim Begrich, *Einleitung in die Psalmen* (Gottingen: Vandenhoeck & Ruprecht, 1933). Claus Westermann, *The Structure of the Book of Job* (Philadelphia: Fortress Press, 1981), employed the structure of the lament as the key to understanding the design of the drama. For him, chapter 31 is an "oath of clearance," a part of a lament that prepares the sufferer to meet God and to be healed and accepted by God.

[3]Nearly every Joban commentator assumes that the speeches of Elihu are intrusive. The nature of the intrusion is discussed differently. Habel, *The Book of Job* (1985), offers the clearest discussion of the design of the Elihu speeches and how that design adds to the plot of the whole work. For Habel, Elihu introduces the third movement of the plot and offers only an apparent

resolution to the drama. But, "contrary to Elihu's predictions, Job's divine adversary does show his face...The Elihu scene is thus a foil, a deliberate anticlimax, which retards the plot and leads the audience to expect a plot development which is the opposite of what really happens" (p. 33). The reader can see how influential Habel's work has been for my own on this point.

⁴There is an enormous literature on the complex issues surrounding the act of reading a text. Two stand out: Wolfgang Iser, *The Act of Reading* (Baltimore, Md.: Johns Hopkins University Press, 1978); and Stanley Fish, *Is There a Text in This Class?* (Cambridge, Mass.: Harvard University Press, 1980). For a delightful and insightful critique of the possible dangers of the implications of Iser and Fish, see Wayne C. Booth, *The Company We Keep* (Berkeley: University of California Press, 1988). For biblical applications of some of the theoretical discussions of Iser and Fish, see, among a host of others, Meir Sternberg, *The Poetics of Biblical Narrative* (Bloomington, Ind.: Indiana University Press, 1985); David M. Gunn and Danna Nolan Fewell, *Narrative in the Hebrew Bible* (New York: Oxford University Press, 1993); Stephen D. Moore, *Literary Criticism and the Gospels* (New Haven, Conn.: Yale University Press, 1989).

Chapter 7: Job 38—42

¹See, for example, Terrien, *The Book of Job*, 1193–94, who emphasizes YHWH's encounter with Job, a meeting that "annihilates his ego, and thus he is able truly to repent." That repentance, says Terrien, is of "the monstrous crime of having condemned his Creator." What YHWH says is subordinate to the simple fact that YHWH comes to Job. Rowley, *Job*, 341, speaks of Job's finding a renewed "fellowship" with God. "For at bottom this was not a problem of theodicy but a problem of fellowship."

²See Habel, *The Book of Job* (1985), 548, for the point.

³For a lyrical portrait of the complexity, cruelty, and wonder of creation, see Annie Dillard, *Pilgrim At Tinker Creek* (New York: Bantam Books, 1974).

⁴Habel, *The Book of Job* (1985), 564.

⁵Pope, *Job*, 320.

⁶Habel, *The Book of Job* (1985), 534.

⁷Ibid., 584.

Chapter 8: "Troubling Physicians Are You All": On Becoming a Joban Preacher

¹Voltaire, *Candide, or Optimism* (New York: Norton, 1991).

²Clines, *Job 1–20*, 294.

³Christine M. Smith, *Preaching as Weeping, Confession, and Resistance* (Louisville: Westminster/John Knox Press, 1992). She summarizes and expands these two challenges in her introduction, "Preaching as a Theological Act," 1–14.

⁴Note my discussion of this question in the commentary and see chapter 4, footnote 1.

⁵Three studies trace the theological struggles of Israel with cogency: Robert Davidson, *The Courage to Doubt* (London: SCM, 1983); Terence E. Fretheim, *The Suffering of God* (Philadelphia: Fortress Press, 1984); W. Lee

Humphreys, *The Tragic Vision and the Hebrew Tradition* (Philadelphia: Fortress Press, 1985). Each of these in unique ways makes it clear that Israel's portrayals of God were far from monolithic and far from comfortable and easily assimilated. The poet of Job stands in a long line of seekers, as these studies demonstrate.

[6]Habel, *The Book of Job* (1985), 583.

Chapter 9: Sermons from Job

[1]See David Buttrick, *Homiletic* (Philadelphia: Fortress Press, 1987); Eugene L. Lowry, *How to Preach a Parable* (Nashville: Abingdon Press, 1989); Ronald J. Allen and John C. Holbert, *Holy Root, Holy Branches* (Nashville: Abingdon Press, 1995).

[2]John C. Holbert, *Preaching Old Testament* (Nashville: Abingdon Press, 1991), 42–45.

[3]Ibid., 42–43.

[4]For a similar kind of sermon, see ibid., "The Best Laugh of All," 79–84.

Commentaries

Clines, David J. A. *Job 1–20*, Word Biblical Commentary, vol. 17. Dallas: Word Books, 1989.

Dhorme, Edouard. *Le Livre de Job*. Paris: J.Gabalda, 1926. Translated by Harold Knight, *A Commentary on the Book of Job*. London: Thomas Nelson and Sons, 1967.

Driver, Samuel Rolles, and Gray, George Buchanan. *A Critical and Exegetical Commentary on the Book of Job*. Edinburgh: T. & T. Clark, 1921.

Fohrer, Georg. *Das Buch Hiob*. Gutersloh: Gerd Mohn, 1963.

Gibson, John C. L. *Job*. Philadelphia: Westminster Press, 1985.

Good, Edwin M. *In Turns of Tempest: A Reading of Job with Translation*. Stanford: Stanford University Press, 1990.

Gordis, Robert. *The Book of Job*. New York: Jewish Theological Seminary of America, 1978.

Habel, Norman C. *The Book of Job*. Cambridge: Cambridge University Press, 1975.

Habel, Norman C. *The Book of Job*. Philadelphia: Westminster Press, 1985.

Hartley, John E. *The Book of Job*. Grand Rapids: Eerdmans, 1988.

Janzen, J. Gerald. *Job*. Atlanta: John Knox, 1985.

Pope, Marvin H. *Job*. Garden City, N.Y.: Doubleday, 1973.

Rowley, H. H. *Job*. London: Thomas Nelson and Sons, 1970.

Selms, A. van. *Job*. Grand Rapids: Eerdmans, 1985.

Terrien, Samuel. *The Book of Job*. Nashville: Abingdon Press, 1954.

Selected Studies

Fohrer, Georg. *Studien zum Buche Hiob*. Gerd Mohn: Gütersloh, 1963.

Frost, Robert. "A Masque of Reason" In *Selected Poems of Robert Frost*, ed. by Robert Graves, pp. 272–88. New York: Holt, Rinehart and Winston, 1963.

Glatzer, Nahum H. *The Dimensions of Job*. New York: Schocken, 1969.

Gordis, Robert. *The Book of God and Man*. Chicago: University of Chicago Press, 1965.

Gutierrez, Gustavo. *On Job*. Maryknoll, N.Y.: Orbis Books, 1987.

Jung, C. G. *Answer to Job*. Princeton, N.J.: Princeton University Press, 1958.

MacLeish, Archibald. *JB*. Boston: Houghton Mifflin, 1956.

Penchansky, David. *The Betrayal of God*. Louisville: Westminster/ John Knox Press, 1990.

Perdue, Leo G., and Gilpin, W. Clark, eds. *The Voice from the Whirlwind*. Nashville: Abingdon Press, 1992.

Polzin, Robert M. *Biblical Structuralism*. Philadelphia: Fortress Press, 1977.

Polzin, Robert, and Robertson, David. *Semeia 7: Studies in the Book of Job*. Missoula: Scholars Press, 1977.

Power, W. J. A. "A Study of Irony in the Book of Job." Ph.D. diss., University of Toronto, 1961.

Reyburn, William D. *A Handbook on the Book of Job*. New York: United Bible Societies, 1992.

Safire, William. *The First Dissident*. New York: Random House, 1992.

Simundson, Daniel J. *The Message of Job*. Minneapolis: Augsburg, 1986.

Spark, Muriel. *The Only Problem*. New York: G. P. Putnam's Sons, 1984.

Westermann, Claus. *The Structure of the Book of Job*. Translated by Charles A. Muenchow. Philadelphia: Fortress Press, 1981.

Wiesel, Elie. "Job, Our Contemporary." In *Messengers of God*. New York: Pocket Books, 1976.